My Testimonies,

Praises and Thanks

Unto the

Lord Jesus Christ

RICKY CLEMONS

PUBLISHED BY FIDELI PUBLISHING, INC.

ISBN: 978-1-962402-67-5

Published by

Fideli Publishing, Inc.
119 W. Morgan St.
Martinsville, IN 46151
www.FideliPublishing.com

Table of Contents

I am So Glad, O Lord

I am so glad, O Lord, that you didn't allow me to be a genius, because I would probably have been full of pride and believed that no one could tell me anything that I didn't already know.

I am so glad, O Lord, that you didn't allow me to be rich, because I would probably have believed I was better than others who were not rich and I would probably have looked down on them like they were nobody.

I am so glad, O Lord, that you didn't allow me to be big, tall and good-looking because I would probably have been having sex with many women and getting some of them pregnant while believing I'm not the father.

I am short, small and of average intelligence man who sometimes struggles with pride, and I believe that if You, O Lord, had allowed me to be a giant of a man I would probably have a mountain of pride like Lucifer and wanted to be god.

I am so glad, O Lord, that you knew what You were doing when you allowed me to not be a giant.

I am so glad, O Lord, that You didn't allow me to have everything, because I would probably have been selfish to the fullest extent and believed that everyone else should pull themselves up by their bootstraps, even though the poor will always be around, just like You said, O Lord.

I am so glad, O Lord, that you didn't allow me to do everything right all the time, because I would probably have been pointing my finger at other people's wrongdoings every day and believing that I was perfect.

Even with all the right that I know today, I still find myself pointing my finger at someone else's wrongdoings, O Lord.

I am so glad, O Lord, that you didn't allow me to be better than anyone else, because I would probably have been comparing myself with those who were less fortunate than me every day, when You, O Lord, didn't create anyone to be a mistake to live in this world where You, O Lord, didn't allow anyone to be lost in their sins without a free will choice.

All that You allowed me to have, O Lord, and all that You allowed me to be, O Lord, is because only You know what is best for me to have, which means I have no reason not to believe in You, O Lord.

I can't speak for anyone else but me, O Lord, because You didn't allow anyone to be lost in their sins without putting Your laws in their hearts so they know some right from wrong and have a conscience — like not eating poison when they know it's poison.

I am so glad, O Lord, that you didn't allow me to destroy myself in my ignorance that tried to make me look so wrong for being alive to have a chance to believe in You, O Lord, and be saved from my ignorant sins.

If I Never

If everything was good in my life, I would believe that I don't' need You, my Lord.

If I never say anything wrong, I would believe that I don't need You, my Lord.

If I never do anything wrong, I would believe that I don't need You, my Lord.

If I never make any mistakes, I would believe that I don't need You, my Lord.

If I never make any bad choices, I would believe that I don't need You, my Lord.

If I knew all things, I would believe that I don't need You, my Lord.

If I could see all things, I would believe that I don't need You, my Lord.

If I could do all things, I would believe that I don't need You, my Lord.

If I never had any hardships, I would believe that I don't need You, my Lord.

I know that I can only speak for myself, because there are many people who don't believe they need You, O Lord, because they are very rich and believe they have no need of You who can take away their riches and wealth.

The angels in heaven are perfect, but they still need You, my Lord and Savior Jesus Christ who created them perfect with a free will to love and obey you forever and ever.

O Lord, You created Adam and Eve perfect, but they stopped believing they needed to always worship you because they desired a fruit that caused them to give the devil dominion over this world.

If everything was perfect in my life, I would believe that I don't need You, my Lord, because I would be like Adam who sinned against You because he believed he was right in his own eyes to eat that fruit.

As I Get Older

As I get older, my life gets better for loving and obeying my Lord and Savior Jesus Christ.

As I get older, my life gets better for trusting Jesus to give me the victory through my trials.

As I get older, my life gets better as I pray to Jesus without ceasing.

As I get older, my life gets better for speaking the Bible truth to people with love.

As I get older, my life gets better for trying my best to eat healthy food because my body belongs to the Lord.

As I get older, my life gets better for making a lot of good choices to please the Lord.

As I get older, my life gets better for not staying up late at night.

As I get older, my life gets better for reading my Bible every day.

As I get older, my life gets better as my faith grows stronger in the Lord.

As I get older, my life gets better for getting a good night's sleep.

As I get older, my life gets better because of my Lord and Savior Jesus Christ who blesses my life.

As I get older, my life gets better for living right unto the Lord.

As I get older, my life gets better because the Lord supplies all of my needs.

As I get older, my life gets better for keeping my eyes on Jesus.

As I get older, my life gets better for returning a faithful tithes and offerings unto Jesus.

As I get older, my life gets better for getting more spiritually mature in Jesus.

As I get older, my life gets better for getting wiser in doing the Lord's will.

As I get older, my life gets better for denying self and picking up my cross to follow Jesus.

As I get older, my life gets better for giving testimonies about what Jesus brought me through.

As I get older, my life gets better for being a witness of Jesus.

As I get older, my life gets better for being like Jesus.

As I get older, my life gets better because Jesus gives me the strength to get through the day.

As I get older, my life gets better for using my spiritual gift to edify the church of Jesus Christ.

As I get older, my life gets better for confessing and repenting of my sins unto Jesus Christ.

Standing Up for the Sabbath

I dreamed about standing up for the Sabbath.

I dreamed that I and my deceased mother were in a place that looked like a small town.

My mother and I walked into a church where we heard some music sounding so divine.

When we entered the church, we saw a woman playing a piano, and another woman was sitting down in the pew.

Yet another woman said out loud, "This man has something to tell you both and it's about keeping the Sabbath day holy." The woman also said, "He's not a preacher."

I said, "I'm a poet and songwriter."

The scene changed and my mother and I were walking together, while she was talking to me.

We walked up to a building that looked like a center where people would go to have activities.

We entered the center and saw some people sitting down.

There was a woman who said with a loud voice, "You all need to listen and hear about the Sabbath."

My mother wanted to sit down, so I pulled out a chair that was between two people.

My mother sat down in the chair and rested.

Then all of a sudden, some police officers rushed into the center and pulled me outside, where they arrested me for standing up for the Sabbath.

I woke up out of my dream and realized that this was a sign of the things that will one day happen to Sabbath day keepers.

So Amazing

One day in the afternoon, I was watching a TV program. On the program was a beautiful young woman flying a plane with her feet because she was born without arms. It was so amazing to me to see that young woman making that great achievement in her life. She had a beautiful smile and she looked so happy as she talked about how she loves to encourage others to do great things.

If that young woman can be so amazing, then what about the Lord who can always do the impossible for you and me.

The Lord Jesus Christ is so amazing. He did amazing things when He lived on earth without sin in His flesh.

The Lord can use anyone to do something amazing.

We can put a limit on someone and believe that he or she doesn't have what it takes to do something amazing. We can do that by believing that we are better and smarter than someone else. We tend to look on the outward appearance of someone who is handicapped mentally or physically.

The Lord sees what that person can become, when you and I can overlook that potential.

The Lord is always amazing to let us live another day.

We have no power to keep ourselves alive if the Lord shuts the door on our lives.

The Lord has blessed that young woman to be so amazing to me, who knows that only the Lord can always do so many new and amazing things to surprise you and me.

Speaking the Truth

One day in the afternoon, I was in a convenience store, standing in line to pay for what I had in my hand.

Before I left the store, I was standing in the checkout line and a man stepped in front of me to pay for what he had in his hand.

Time stood still.

I said to the man, "I was in front of you," and he told me to go ahead.

I looked at him and he looked at me as we stood there frozen in our footsteps.

I knew that I was in line ahead of him and he knew it too.

I don't think that I sinned against the Lord when I spoke the truth to that man.

I was not angry with him for getting in front of me.

I am glad he didn't have a hot temper.

I could have stood there and said nothing at all, but I chose to speak the truth.

The man accepted the truth in front of me and the other people in the store.

I thank the Lord that there was some good in him to let me check out before him.

Speaking the truth has got many people killed.

Speaking the truth can cause me and you to have many enemies who will get revenge at us for speaking the truth that they hate.

Jesus has always spoken the truth, even though he made many enemies who didn't accept the truth that is Jesus Christ.

Speaking the truth, especially in love, can surely change someone's life for the better.

Someone Asked Me

Someone asked me, "Do you have the holy ghost?"

I said, "Yes, because I believe in Jesus Christ, who is the most positive influence in my life from day to day."

I must believe in Jesus to have the Holy Ghost as I pray to Jesus to give me His holy ghost.

The Holy Ghost teaches me the truth about Jesus, who I can always boast about because He is worthy of all the glory and praise.

If anyone believes in Jesus Christ, they have the Holy Ghost who testifies of Jesus Christ in His holy word.

His word is all truth to set us free from lies in this life.

You and I can't have the Holy Ghost if we don't believe in Jesus Christ, who is God's only begotten Son.

He relieved us from being lost in our sins.

Jesus can save us from our sins and fill us with His holy ghost for believing in him.

He sent the Holy Ghost to this world after He left it and went back to heaven to be with God.

Someone asked me, "Do you have the Holy Ghost?"

I said, "Yes, I do," and I felt so free.

The Only Way
That I can be a Christian

The only way that I can be a Christian is to be like you, my Lord and Savior Jesus Christ.

Being a Christian is being like you, O Lord.

I don't want to be a mean Christian.

I don't want to be a proud Christian.

I don't want to be a show-off Christian.

The only way that I can be a Christian is to be like you, my Lord and Savior Jesus Christ.

I don't want to be a high-minded Christian.

I don't want to be a sad Christian.

I don't want to be a gossiping Christian.

I don't want to be a gluttonous Christian.

I don't want to be in a discontent Christian.

I don't want to be a greedy Christian.

The only way that I can be a Christian is to be like you, my Lord and Savior Jesus Christ.

I don't want to be a lying Christian.

I don't want to be an unforgiving Christian.

I don't want to be a revengeful Christian.

I don't want to be a troublemaker Christian.

The only way that I can be a Christian is to be like you, my Lord and Savior Jesus Christ.

I don't want to be a hypocrite Christian.

I don't want to be a favoritism Christian.

I don't want to be a manipulating Christian.

I don't want to be a deceptive Christian.

I don't want to be an unbalanced Christian.

I don't want to be an unstable Christian.

I don't want to be an ignorant Christian.

The only way that I can be a Christian is to be like you, my Lord and Savior Jesus Christ.

I don't want to be a lawbreaker Christian.

I don't want to be a judgmental Christian.

I don't want to be a careless Christian.

I don't want to be an impolite Christian.

I don't want to be a selfish Christian.

I don't want to be a discouraging Christian.

Many people go to church and believe that they are Christians, but instead they're being like the devil in the presence of many people who believe that a Christian can talk any kind of way, act any kind of way, and dress any kind of way and still be called a Christian.

The only way to be a Christian is to be like you, my Lord and Savior Jesus Christ, who lived on earth without sin to be the right example for a Christian to be like every day.

I Love My Church Family

My church family is not made up of perfect people, but I love my church family.

I love to be in church with my church family.

I love to worship the Lord with my church family.

I love to pray with my church family.

I love to have Bible studies with my church family.

I love to fellowship with my church family.

I love talking to my church family.

The Lord has blessed me with a good church family.

The Lord has brought me a long way with my church family.

My church family is a blessing from the Lord.

My brothers and sisters in the Lord are not perfect people, but I am glad that they are in my life.

My church family helps me to hold onto my Lord Jesus Christ.

My church family helps me to love and obey the Lord.

I want to make it to heaven with my church family.

I love my church family, regardless of them falling short of the glory of God.

My church family and I have come a long way in the Lord.

I love being on one accord with my church family.

I love praying for my church family.

It's an honor and a privilege to go through some trials with my church family.

I want to always be in my church family's lives.

I don't want to ever turn my back on my church family.

I know that my church family is a gift to me from the Lord.

My brothers and sisters in the Lord help me to keep my eyes on the Lord Jesus Christ.

My church family helps me to keep myself humble unto the Lord.

I love growing stronger in the Lord with my church family.

I love holding onto my church family.

My church family is not made up of perfect people, but they are trying their best to love and obey the Lord.

My church family is not made up of perfect people, but they are trying their best to love me even though they can see I am far from being perfect.

My church family helps me to make Jesus my choice every day.

My church family is a small family, but they are strong in the Lord.

My church family knows that this world is not their home.

They know that they are pilgrims passing through this old sinful world.

My church family encourages me and reminds me that I am a pilgrim like them, just passing through this world to get to our destination in heaven one day.

Living in Paradise

I believed that I was living in paradise when I was in the army and stationed in Hawaii.

I remember when I was flying in the United 747 aircraft and looked out the window and saw the beautiful green hills and waterfalls.

I also remember seeing the beautiful navy blue pacific ocean waters that captivated my attention during my flight to Hawaii.

I believed that I was living in paradise when I got on the bus leaving Scofield barracks and going to Waikiki with my friends on the weekends when I was off-duty.

Waikiki was like a paradise with beautiful Hawaiian women looking like heaven on earth, along with the mystical park sitting so close to the beautiful white beach sand.

The Hawaiian native Samoan men and women were friendly and like angels on earth to me.

They were so good to be around and smoke pot with.

I wasn't a Christian at that time, but I truly felt like I was in heaven on earth when I was stationed in Hawaii.

That was the most beautiful place I have been to in my life.

If Hawaii can be like a paradise and other places here on earth can too, then what about the real paradise in Heaven that Jesus wants to take us to when He comes back again?

We just can't imagine what heaven is like, but we can be very sure that heaven is a paradise where there is no sin.

God will create a new heaven and a new earth that will be paradise for all who are saved in Jesus Christ who is paradise to our souls for being saved in Him.

Paradise would not be paradise without Jesus, who allowed Hawaii to be like a paradise as well as other tropical islands that belong to Jesus, who also owns all the world, all the heavens and all the other worlds.

Pray Without Ceasing

The Lord says to pray without ceasing because the Lord knows better than you and me that prayer is very powerful.

The Lord says to pray without ceasing, and that truly always works for our good because we just don't know when the evil will come our way on any day.

Whenever I leave my house and get in my car, I pray to the Lord to help me to represent Him while I drive on the road.

I also pray to the Lord to help me to represent Him in the store where I shop for food.

One beautiful, sunny, warm day, I went to the store and when I went inside the Walmart store I heard a man talking close behind me.

I didn't look behind me to see if he was talking to someone on the phone, so I kept on walking while taking my time to get to the lane where I needed to go.

The young man who was close behind me had a grocery cart that he pushed up on the back of my left foot.

I stopped walking and quickly looked around at him with an angry look on my face as I said to him, "Look where you're going."

The young man said to me, "I am sorry," and then he touched my left arm and said you are a good man.

I was still a little angry at him and I said to him, "I thank the Lord," so he would know that it's the Lord who kept me in control of myself.

The young man recognized the Lord in me.

I truly believe that if I had not prayed to the Lord before I entered the Walmart store, then the situation would not have turned out good for me and him.

The Lord loves us both the same.

It's always good to pray without ceasing because prayer can surely keep you and me strong in the Lord when the devil tries his best to make trouble for us and make us angry at people who may not intentionally harm us.

Even if people intentionally do us wrong, prayer is still very powerful to keep us strong in the Lord and keep us calm so we make the devil angry that he didn't succeed in causing you and me to misrepresent the Lord in the presence of especially unbelievers.

I Want to Keep My Eyes on Jesus

I don't want to keep my eyes on people who make mistakes.

I want to keep my eyes on Jesus; He makes no mistakes.

I don't want to keep my eyes on people who have flaws.

I want to keep my eyes on Jesus, who has no flaws.

I don't want to keep my eyes on people who can say something wrong.

I want to keep my eyes on Jesus, who can't say anything wrong.

I don't want to keep my eyes on people who can do something wrong.

I want to keep my eyes on Jesus, who can't do anything wrong.

I don't want to keep my eyes on people who I can't put all my trust in.

I want to keep my eyes on Jesus, who I can put all my trust in.

I don't want to keep my eyes on people who can let me down.

I want to keep my eyes on Jesus, who will never let me down.

I don't want to keep my eyes on people who can tell me a lie.

I want to keep my eyes on Jesus, who can't lie to me.

I don't want to keep my eyes on people who can deceive me.

I want to keep my eyes on Jesus, who will never deceive me.

I don't want to keep my eyes on people who can disappoint me.

I want to keep my eyes on Jesus, who will never disappoint me.

I don't want to keep my eyes on people who can talk bad about me.

I want to keep my eyes on Jesus, who will never talk bad about me.

I don't want to keep my eyes on people who can lie about me.

I want to keep my eyes on Jesus, who will never lie about me.

I don't want to keep my eyes on people who can cheat me.

I want to keep my eyes on Jesus, who will never cheat me.

I don't want to keep my eyes on people who can use me.

I want to keep my eyes on Jesus, who will never use me.

I don't want to keep my eyes on people who can hate me.

I want to keep my eyes on Jesus, who will never hate me.

I don't want to keep my eyes on people who can dislike me.

I want to keep my eyes on Jesus, who will never dislike me.

I don't want to keep my eyes on people who can fail me.

I want to keep my eyes on Jesus, who will never fail me.

I don't want to keep my eyes on people who can give me injustice.

I want to keep my eyes on Jesus, who will always give me justice.

I don't want to keep my eyes on people who can misunderstand me.

I want to keep my eyes on Jesus, who will never misunderstand me.

I don't want to keep my eyes on people who can kill me.

I want to keep my eyes on Jesus, who will never kill me.

I don't want to keep my eyes on people who can steal from me.

I want to keep my eyes on Jesus who will never steal from me.

I don't want to keep my eyes on people who can hurt me.

I want to keep my eyes on Jesus who will never hurt me.

I don't want to keep my eyes on people who can be opinionated about me.

I want to keep my eyes on Jesus, who will never be opinionated about me.

I don't want to keep my eyes on people who can change on me.

I want to keep my eyes on Jesus, who will never change on me.

I don't want to keep my eyes on people who can leave me or forsake me.

I want to keep my eyes on Jesus, who will never leave me or forsake me.

I don't want to keep my eyes on people who can reject me.

I want to keep my eyes on Jesus, who will never reject me.

I don't want to keep my eyes on people who can take me the wrong way.

I want to keep my eyes on Jesus, who will never take me the wrong way.

I don't want to keep my eyes on people who can ignore me.

I want to keep my eyes on Jesus, who will never ignore me.

I don't want to keep my eyes on people who can trick me.

I want to keep my eyes on Jesus, who will never trick me.

I don't want to keep my eyes on people who can want to control me.

I want to keep my eyes on Jesus, who will never control me.

I don't want to keep my eyes on people who can want to fight me.

I want to keep my eyes on Jesus, who will never fight me.

I don't want to keep my eyes on people who may not be real with me.

I want to keep my eyes on Jesus, who is always real with me.

I don't want to keep my eyes on people who can see me and can act like they don't see me.

I want to keep my eyes on Jesus, who sees me and lets me know that He sees me.

I don't want to keep my eyes on people who can hear me and can act like they don't hear me.

I want to keep my eyes on Jesus, who hears me and lets me know that He hears me.

I don't want to keep my eyes on people who can oppress me.

I want to keep my eyes on Jesus, who will never oppress me.

I don't want to keep my eyes on people who can depress me.

I want to keep my eyes on Jesus, who can never depress me.

I don't want to keep my eyes on people who can cause me to get sick.

I want to keep my eyes on Jesus, who will never cause me to get sick.

I don't want to keep my eyes on people who are not perfect.

I want to keep my eyes on Jesus, who is perfect and without sin.

I don't want to keep my eyes on people who have sins to confess and repent of.

I want to keep my eyes on Jesus, who can save me from my sins.

I don't want to keep my eyes on people who have no heaven to put me in.

I want to keep my eyes on Jesus, who has a heaven to put me in.

I don't want to keep my eyes on people who can mess things up.

I want to keep my eyes on Jesus, who will never mess anything up.

I don't want to keep my eyes on people who can set me up for a fall.

I want to keep my eyes on Jesus, who will never set me up for a fall.

I don't want to keep my eyes on people who can be jealous of me.

I want to keep my eyes on Jesus, who wants to give me the best.

I don't want to keep my eyes on people who can act like they're better than me.

I want to keep my eyes on Jesus, who created me wonderfully made in His image.

I want to always keep my eyes on Jesus Christ, my Lord and Savior.

I don't want to keep my eyes on people who can pretend to be something they are not.

I don't want to keep my eyes on people who can mock me.

I want to keep my eyes on Jesus, who will never mock me.

I don't want to keep my eyes on people who can break my heart.

I want to keep my eyes on Jesus, who will never break my heart.

I don't want to keep my eyes on people who can tell me one thing and then do another thing.

I want to keep my eyes on Jesus, who will do what He tells me He will do.

I don't want to keep my eyes on people who can try to make me look bad.

I want to keep my eyes on Jesus, who makes me look good for doing His will.

I don't want to keep my eyes on people who can give me evil eye looks.

I want to keep my eyes on Jesus, who gives me His kind looks of mercy.

I don't want to keep my eyes on people who can ruin my reputation.

I want to keep my eyes on Jesus, who gives me a good reputation for loving Him and keeping His Commandments.

I don't want to keep my eyes on people who may not care anything about what I'm doing for the Lord.

I want to keep my eyes on Jesus, who always cares about what I am doing in His holy name.

I don't want to keep my eyes on people who can condemn me to Hell.

I want to keep my eyes on Jesus, who wants to save me from being lost in Hell.

I don't want to keep my eyes on people who can betray me.

I want to keep my eyes on Jesus, who will never betray me.

I don't want to keep my eyes on people who can laugh at me.

I want to keep my eyes on Jesus, who will never laugh at me.

I don't want to keep my eyes on people who can cause me to sin.

I want to keep my eyes on Jesus, who wants to cleanse me from my sins.

I don't want to keep my eyes on people who can twist their words up on me.

I want to keep my eyes on Jesus, who makes His words straight with me.

I don't want to keep my eyes on people who can confuse me.

I want to keep my eyes on Jesus, who will never confuse me.

I don't want to keep my eyes on people who can plot evil things against me.

I want to keep my eyes on Jesus, who is good to me all the time.

I don't want to keep my eyes on people who may not be true to me.

I want to keep my eyes on Jesus, who is always true to me.

I don't want to keep my eyes on people who may try to butter me up to do what they want me to do

I want to keep my eyes on Jesus, who will tell me like it is and let me choose to do what He wants me to do.

O Lord, Help Me

O Lord, help me to not lie to anyone.

O Lord, help me to not lie on anyone.

O Lord, help me to not steal from anyone.

O Lord, help me to not kill anyone.

O Lord, help me to not to cheat anyone.

O Lord, help me to not hurt anyone.

O Lord, help me to not abuse anyone.

O Lord, help me to not use anyone.

O Lord, help me to not to be jealous of anyone.

O Lord, help me to not to envy anyone.

O Lord, help me to not want what belongs to someone else.

O Lord, help me to not put anyone down.

O Lord, help me to not talk bad about anyone.

O Lord, help me to not treat anyone bad.

O Lord, help me to not hate anyone.

O Lord, help me to not disrespect anyone.

O Lord, help me to not be rude to anyone.

O Lord, help me to not give anyone a bad name.

O Lord, help me to not ruin anyone's name.

O Lord, help me to not discourage anyone.

O Lord, help me to not disappoint anyone.

O Lord, help me to not judge anyone.

O Lord, help me to not deceive anyone.

O Lord, help me to not give anyone an evil eye look.

O Lord, help me to not get revenge back at anyone.

O Lord, help me to not hold grudges against anyone.

O Lord, help me to not trick anyone.

O Lord, help me to not try to control anyone.

O Lord, help me to not care less about anyone.

O Lord, help me to not be mean to anyone.

O Lord, help me to not make trouble for anyone.

O Lord, help me to not quarrel with anyone.

O Lord, help me to not fight with anyone.

O Lord, help me to not treat anyone unfairly.

O Lord, help me to not neglect anyone.

O Lord, help me to not show favoritism to anyone.

O Lord, help me to not cause anyone to stumble into sin.

O Lord, help me to not cause anyone to leave the church.

O Lord, help me to not cause anyone to be lost in their sins.

O Lord, you command me to love my neighbor, as I love myself.

Everybody in the church is my neighbor and everybody in this world is my neighbor, who you, O Lord, command me to love.

O Lord, help me to not be impolite to anyone.

O Lord, help me to not believe that I am better than anyone else.

O Lord, help me to not cause anyone to get ill.

O Lord, help me to love you and love my neighbors for me to love myself.

The Power of the Holy Ghost

I dreamed about a man I had prayed for. I dreamed that I was in a building filled with people I didn't know.

We were all sitting down and talking.

Then, all of a sudden, this one man that I knew asked me if I would pray for him because he had cancer.

He walked over to my table and I stood up and took off my hat, then I began to pray for him.

As I was praying, I was a little fearful of the crowd of people.

I continued to pray despite the fear, and the man and the crowd started praying along with me.

Then, the power of the Holy Ghost filled the place as I laid my hand on the man's head while I kept praying for him.

My prayer got louder and louder as did the prayers from the crowd.

I felt the power of the Holy Ghost moving all over the place.

As I continued to pray, some church members walked into the building.

They were surprised to see me praying in front of a large crowd of people.

The Lord was with me, the ill man and the people in the crowd who loved the Lord Jesus Christ with the power of His Holy Ghost.

You Show Mercy on Me

I don't deserve to have any good things from You, O Lord.

You show mercy on me and give me good things.

I deserve to die in my sins.

You show mercy on me, O Lord, and forgive me of my sins.

I don't deserve to be alive.

You show mercy on me, my Lord Jesus Christ, and let me live another day.

I don't deserve any of Your blessings.

You show mercy on me, my Lord, and bless me.

I don't deserve Your love, my Lord.

You show mercy on me and give me Your everlasting love.

I don't deserve to talk to You, my Lord.

You show mercy on me and listen to what I say to You.

I don't deserve to ask You for anything, O Lord.

You show mercy on me and answer my prayers.

I don't deserve to have a relationship with You, my Lord.

You show mercy on me and have a relationship with me.

I don't deserve to call on Your holy name, my Lord Jesus Christ.

You show mercy on me and give me power and the victory in Your name.

I Have Nothing to Complain About

I have nothing to complain about when there are people who are blind and can't see.

I have nothing to complain about when there are people who can't hear anything.

I have nothing to complain about when there are people who have no arms and hands.

I have nothing to complain about when there are people who are paralyzed.

I have nothing to complain about when there are people who have no legs.

I have nothing to complain about when there are people who have no feet.

I have nothing to complain about when there are people who have no houses to live in.

I have nothing to complain about when there are people who have no cars to drive.

I have nothing to complain about when there are people who have no jobs.

I have nothing to complain about when there are people who can't breathe on their own.

I have nothing to complain about when there are people who have lost their businesses.

I have nothing to complain about when there are people who have lost their minds.

I have nothing to complain about when there are people who have lost everything they owned.

I have nothing to complain about when there are people who have taken their own lives.

I have nothing to complain about when there are people who have lost their memories.

I have nothing to complain about when there are people who can't talk.

I have nothing to complain about when there are people whose dreams have been crushed.

I have nothing to complain about when there are people who have been abused and haven't been healed.

I have nothing to complain about when there are people who have lost loved ones and can't move on.

I have nothing to complain about when there are people who have no food to eat.

I have nothing to complain about when there are people who have no clean water to drink.

I have nothing to complain about when there are people who are dying right now.

I have nothing to complain about when there are people who can tell me that I have it good.

I have nothing to complain about when there are people who can tell me that I am rich.

I have nothing to complain about when there are people who can tell me that I'm not going through much of anything at all.

I have nothing to complain about when there are people who can tell me that I have nothing to complain about.

Complaining cannot solve problems.

Complaining can make problems much worse.

Complaining can cause your blood pressure to go up.

Complaining can cause us to not get a good night's sleep.

Complaining can cause us to get weary.

Complaining will make us feel discontent.

Complaining will cause us to not put our trust in the Lord.

Complaining will cause us to displease the Lord.

Complaining can cause us to not have faith in the Lord.

Complaining can call us to stray away from the Lord.

Complaining has caused many marriages to fail.

Complaining is of the devil who complained about God to the angels in heaven.

I have nothing to complain about when I don't deserve to be alive today that the Lord is my hope, and I am thankful unto Him for bringing me this far in my life.

I Wrestled with the Lord

I wrestled with the Lord all night long in my mind.

I had a lot of things on my mind that I needed to talk to the Lord about.

I talked to the Lord about my family.

I talk to the Lord about my kinfolks.

I talked to the Lord about my church family.

I talked to the Lord about my next-door neighbors.

I talked to the Lord about this nation's leaders.

I talked to the Lord about my friends.

I talked to the Lord about myself.

I had a real good talk with the Lord, all night long.

My good Lord Jesus Christ listened to what I had to say to Him.

The more I talked to the Lord, the more I didn't want to stop talking.

I wrestled with the Lord all night long in my mind, until He blessed me.

My Lord Jesus Christ blessed me in my mind.

He gave me peace of mind.

He answered my prayers in the early morning sunlight.

I didn't let the Lord go in my mind until I knew I felt much better in the early morning sunlight, then I finally got some sleep.

I wrestled with the Lord all night long in my mind that was heavy with the things that I have no control over.

I wrestled with the Lord all night long in my mind that was heavy with the uncertainty of life.

The Lord blessed my mind and took away the heavy burdens in my mind.

I am so glad that I chose to not let Jesus go as I wrestled with Jesus all night long.

Jesus strengthened my mind and cleansed my mind from filthy things of the world.

I felt so brand new in my mind because I didn't let my Lord Jesus go as I wrestled with Him all night long and He blessed me.

In the Army of God

In the Army, I was trained for physical fitness so that I would be sent to fight in a war.

In the Army, I was trained to tie different knots.

In the Army, I was trained to put up barbed wire fences.

In the Army, I was trained to armed and disarmed in M-15 anti-tank mines.

In the Army, I was trained to set up M-19 anti-personnel mines.

In the Army, I was trained to set up Claymore mines.

In the Army, I was trained to sweep land with a mine detector.

In the Army, I was trained to probe mines.

In the Army, I was trained to fire an M-16 machine gun.

In the Army, I was trained to fire an M-203 grenade launcher.

In the Army, I was trained to fire an M-72 rocket launcher.

In the Army, I was trained to fire an M-60 machine gun.

In the Army, I was trained to throw a hand grenade.

In the Army, I was trained to detect radiation.

In the Army I was trained to be a radio operator.

In the Army, I was trained to fight in a war that I never got a chance to fight in.

Every soldier must be trained to fight to the death.

Many soldiers have died, even though they had good training that was not 100% perfectly guaranteed to protect every soldier from being killed.

Today, I am in the army of God, fighting against spiritual wickedness that loves to shoot bullets of lies at me.

Today, I am in the army of God, fighting against spiritual wickedness that loves to throw grenades of rebellion at me.

Today, I am in the army of God, fighting against spiritual wickedness that loves to blast off its mines of deceptions at me.

Today, I am in the army of God, fighting against spiritual wickedness that loves to drop its bombs of hatred on me.

Today, I am in the army of God, fighting against spiritual wickedness that loves to spread its radiation of injustice upon me.

There are no spiritual casualties in God's Army that is equipped for every soldier to fight against spiritual wickedness.

Jesus Christ, our Lord and Savior, is the top general of God's Army.

Jesus gives us the command to win the spiritual war by loving Him and keeping His Commandments so that spiritual wickedness will never be able to win the war against God.

I am a Christian Black Man

I am a Christian Black man with a dream to lead me through an opinionated world of me existing because of God's love for me.

I am a Christian Black man to face up to myself to love or hate who I am.

This world will stress out my existence from day to day.

I can only be me and love or hate myself in the presence of opinionated people who don't know me.

I am a Christian Black man who is not here by accident.

God came up with a good idea to create me like He wanted to.

God didn't make a mistake when the devil made a mistake to judge me and hate me who can choose to love God and my neighbors.

The devil is my true enemy.

He knows that God didn't create me to be an empty shell.

The sand can run out of an hourglass.

A star can fall from the sky.

A shadow can disappear.

I am a Christian Black man who God created for eternity beyond the things that are temporary and can end.

I am a Christian Black man who can love everybody, even though some people hate me.

I am somebody to God, even if nobody else cares.

I am a human being who God created in His image, and I think, reason and live to worship Him.

I am not an animal that can't think and can't reason things out.

When you see me, you can see that I am a human being like you.

You may want to hate me or kill me for no good reason, even though you may believe you have a good reason.

I am a Christian Black man all day and all night long.

My color won't change for you, even if you have a problem with the color of my skin.

Jesus Christ, my Lord and Savior, died on the cross for my sins too.

He didn't leave me out of His salvation because I am black.

When you see me in heaven, don't be shocked.

Heaven is for the Christian black man too.

I love who I am, and I am black, not Asian, Jewish, white or Arab, or any other race.

If you have a problem with me being black, then you need to talk to God about it.

I am a Christian Black man who was born to be black.

Life welcomes me into this world because I was meant to be here to do God's will.

Being black is a problem for anyone who doesn't love God.

God says that if you say you love Him who you don't see but hate your brother who you do see, then you are a liar.

I am your black brother who you do see.

I am a Christian Black man existing to live in a sinful world where the devil is my real, true enemy who tries to cause my soul to be lost.

I am a Christian Black man walking through the wilderness of the uncertain that loves to try to make me think living my life is in vain.

God has made my life worth living to be like the sound of gospel songs.

My blackness will follow me wherever I go.

It will attract some attention, and some will accept me for being black.

I am a Christian Black man who is a controversial subject to the devil.

He knows that if I love Jesus Christ, he lost his victory over me.

I am a Christian Black man who is no island sitting all alone in the middle of the sea.

God will stand me up in the middle of his angels every day.

God created me to be a black man who he approves of in this world and in the new world to come one day.

Could it be profound to God to create a black man to be different from all other men of different races?

God is matchless, so who can question God for creating a black man like me?

I am a Christian Black man who is tossed on every side of the world by people stereotyping me like poisonous fumes coming out of an exhaust pipe.

My Lord and Savior Jesus Christ has renewed my life for me.

His love is just like clean air to breathe in and out day after day.

Ignorance will conspire against me and injustice will gladly accuse me of being a Christian black man day after day in a world that shows favoritism to the privileged.

I am a Christian Black man who God favors to live in this world and claim my existence.

I am a Christian Black man who the sun will shine down on with respect.

The full white moon will glow down on me with respect.

The rainbow will arch up high over me with respect.

The rain and snow will fall down on me with respect.

Nature will surround me with respect.

Nature will treat me as no less of a man than any other man of any race, creed or culture of men.

I am a Christian Black man for others to see and greatly accept when Jesus comes back again.

You Didn't Cast Me Out

I am so glad, O Lord, that You didn't cast me out when I came to You with a tormented mind.

O Lord, you set me free from a tormented mind so I could worship You and give you all the praise and glory.

O Lord, you didn't cast me out when I came to You all broken up in shame and guilt.

O Lord, you didn't cast me out when I came to You with an unclean spirit that tortured my soul day and night.

I am so glad, O Lord, that you didn't cast me out when I came to You with a sincere heart to want to give up the things that failed me.

O Lord, you didn't cast me out when I came to you with nothing good in me — You accepted me with joy and changed my life to do Your holy will.

Oh Lord, you didn't cast me out when I came to You so messed up in sin that You set me free from living in.

O Lord, you didn't cast me out when I came to You with my ignorance that you winked your eye at.

O Lord, you didn't cast me out when I came to You with my weakness that you strengthened for me to resist the devil's temptations.

O Lord, you didn't cast me out when I came to You with a little, simple prayer — You looked down on me and answered my prayers from heaven above.

O Lord, you didn't cast me out when I came to you in my poor spirit — You made my spirit rich so that I could be a witness of You to all the world.

I Thank You, O Lord

I thank You, O Lord, for looking down on me from up in Your heavens on high.

I thank You, O Lord, for spending some time with me, who is nowhere near to Your all-knowing mind and all-seeing eyes.

O Lord God, You sent Your only begotten Son, Jesus Christ, to this sinful world to save me from my sins as if I was the only sinner living among billions of other perfect people in this world.

O Lord, my God, you know all of my heart that I will never know like You, who always knows how to make me feel so loved by You.

I thank You, O Lord, for taking the time to talk to me and listen to me who you see to be Your child who is longing for Your Holy Spirit to live in me day after day.

O my Lord God, You are all present and all around me day after day.

I see You in good Christian people, in nature and most of all I see You, my Lord God, in Your holy word that is filled with nothing but the truth about You.

O my Lord God, I thank you for looking down on poor little me who You want to be in heaven with You when You send Your Son, Jesus Christ, back to this world again to take me to heaven as if I was the only one here on earth.

I thank you, O Lord, for looking down on me from heaven and giving me Your extended time for me to truly know that it's You who kept me alive to see this day that I have no excuse to not love You and keep Your Commandments.

O Lord, You have brushed off my ignorance through Your holy word that is all truth about You for me to live my life unto You with my conscience awakened in making You my choice every day, O my Lord God.

Who Am I to Question You, O Lord?

Who am I to question You, O Lord, about why You allow bad things to happen in this world?

Who am I to question You, O Lord, about why You allow good people to suffer hardships?

Who am I to question You, O Lord, about why You allow many young people to die?

Who am I to question You, O Lord, about why You allow my enemies to degrade me?

Who am I to question You, O Lord, about why You allow the rich to get richer and the poor to get poorer?

Who am I to question You, O Lord, about why You allow the wheat and tares in the church to grow together?

Who am I to question You, O Lord, about why You haven't come back yet?

Who am I to question You, O Lord, about why I have to put up with some selfish and proud church folks?

Who am I to question You, O Lord, about why You allowed me to make it this far in life?

Who am I to question You, O Lord, about why You even put up with me?

Who am I to question You, O Lord, about why You allow some criminals to get away with their crimes?

Who am I to question You, O Lord, about why You allow many people to be prejudiced against another race of people?

Who am I to question You, O Lord, about why You allow many innocent children, women and men to get killed in war?

Who am I to question You, O Lord, about why You allow many people to break the laws of the land?

Who am I to question You, O Lord, about why You allowed sinful men to crucify You on the cross?

Who am I to question You, O Lord, about what You said to Job: "Where were you when I laid down the foundations of the earth?"

Job got his answer from the Lord God, whose answer was so profound to Job that he never questioned God again.

God questioned Job, but Job couldn't give God a good answer to His question.

This goes to show that God always knows what to do for our soul's salvation in Him through his Son, Jesus Christ, who existed before anything in heaven and on earth.

Who am I to question You, O Lord, who sees all things, knows all things and can do all things when I can be questioned and have no answer to give?

It's Always Good to do Right

It's always good to do right, even if you think no one sees you doing right.

One morning, I went to the Walmart store to buy a loaf of bread.

When I walked up to the self-checkout machine, I used my bank Visa card to pay for the bread.

As I was using my card, some coins came out of the machine— quarters, dimes, nickels and pennies.

The devil tried to tempt me to keep those coins for myself, but the Lord spoke to me to tell the clerk that the machine was giving out coins that didn't belong to me.

I obeyed the voice of the Lord and left those coins in the cup on the machine.

I am so glad I did the right thing and didn't do what the devil wanted me to do.

The devil didn't want me to be like Jesus in the Walmart store, where people could see who is like Jesus and who is not like Jesus.

Jesus Christ is our righteous Lord and our righteous Savior who does everything right from now until eternity.

It's always good to do right, even if no one else is around to see you because God sees everything you and I do.

God will judge us whether we are doing right or wrong.

The Lord is Still Working with Me

The Lord is still working with me, who is not always easy to work with and can sometimes be a pain in the neck for the Lord.

The Lord is still working with me, and the Lord Jesus Christ shows me that he is working things out in my life.

The Lord is still working with me, regardless of me not always trusting Him to show me what I need to see in my life to draw closer to Him.

The Lord is still working with me, who has a slim chance of making it to heaven because I don't always love and obey Him with my whole heart.

The Lord is still working with me, who is a winner who He wants to save in His amazing grace.

The Lord is still working with me, who doesn't know what a day will bring me when the Lord knows before I can say one word.

The Lord is still working with me, and will continue to do so until I go to the grave.

I hope to be saved in Jesus before I go to the grave and sleep away to one day awake and see Jesus on the clouds of glory.

The Good Things that I Do

The good things that I do I want them to glorify Your holy name, my Lord Jesus Christ.

I don't want to glorify my name that has spots and blemishes.

The good things that I do I want them to be all about You, my Lord and savior Jesus Christ.

I don't want them to be all about me, who can make mistakes in my name.

The good things that I do I want them to be about Your business, my Lord Jesus Christ.

I don't want them to be about my business that can go out of business in my name.

The good things that I do I want them to win souls to You, my Lord Jesus Christ.

I don't want them to win souls to me, who has sins to confess and repent of unto You, my Lord.

The good things that I do I want them to draw people to You, my Lord Jesus Christ.

I don't want them to draw people to me, who can pull away from You, my Lord, in ways that I don't see.

The good things that I do I want them to honor Your holy name, my Lord.

I don't want them to honor my name, which has been dishonored through some bad choices that I made.

I Know that I Will Be Blessed

I know that I will be blessed when I walk through the church doors to enter the church that's filled with ministry works.

I know that I will be blessed when I hear the Sabbath school lesson being taught by the Sabbath school teacher giving a good message about Jesus Christ, my Lord and savior.

I know that I will be blessed when I get a hug from my brothers and sisters who will never mug me.

I know that I will be blessed when I hear a children's story being told to the little children who are so much more precious than gold.

I know that I will be blessed when I hear a song that someone sings about my Lord Jesus who will never do me wrong.

I know that I will be blessed when I hear a sermon about my Lord Jesus Christ who I have no reason to ever doubt.

I know that I will be blessed when I see my sisters and brothers worshipping the Lord and loving one another.

I know that I will be blessed for being in the household of faith where I can lay down all of my burdens to Jesus Christ on the holy Sabbath day of rest.

I know that I will be blessed to feel the Holy Spirit beyond words to say.

You are Cleansing Me from My Sins

O Lord, you are cleansing me from my sins.

I don't want to do those sinful things that I used to do.

O Lord, you are cleansing me from my sins.

I have no desire to do those sinful things that I used to do.

O Lord, you are cleansing me from my sins.

I don't do many of those sinful things that I used to do.

I confess my sins and I repent of my sins unto You, my Lord and savior Jesus Christ.

You shed your precious blood on the cross to cleanse me from my sins and to save me from my sins.

I am very aware of my seen sins. I want You, my Lord, to cleanse me of these because I want to be saved in You, my Lord.

You will show me my unseen sins that I want to repent of unto You.

O Lord, I don't want to sin against You in words and in what I do, even though I am not without sin.

You are cleansing me from my sins, O Lord, because of my confessions and repentance unto You.

I don't want to deliberately sin against You.

There is Nothing You Can't Do

There is nothing you can't do for me, O Lord.

I can put all of my trust in You who sees and foresees my future days that are in Your almighty hands.

If it's in Your will, O Lord, I will see those future days in the land of the living.

There is nothing that you can't do for me, Lord Jesus.

You have brought me through all of my past days that I don't deserve, and I am so glad to see this day and to be alive.

The devil is so mad when he sees me doing so well, especially in doing Your will, O Lord.

You can't fail me, from my birth to my old age that is a blessing from you, my Lord and Savior Jesus Christ.

There is nothing that You can't do for me in my life, O Lord who will supply all of my needs.

I don't have to worry about anything, because nothing is too hard for You to see and no problem too difficult for You to solve.

There is nothing that You can't do for me, O Lord, even if I am on my dying bed.

I know that I will one day live again when you come back.

Help Me to Represent You

Help me represent You, my Lord and Savior Jesus Christ.

I want to represent You, O Lord, so people will see you in my life wherever I go here and there.

Help me to represent You, so people will see You in my eyes because they get no judgmental looks from me.

Help me to represent You, O Lord, in what I say to people so they hear kind words from the tip of my tongue every day.

Help me to represent You, my Lord, in what I do, so that my actions will be about You and represent You all through my life.

When people look at me, I want them to see You, O Lord, who can set anyone free from being selfish.

O Lord, You brought me a long way so I could see this day and love You and my neighbors.

I want to represent You, my Lord Jesus, who's always able to change my heart so I can confess and repent of my sins.

Help me to represent You, O Lord, even when I just don't know what effect I will have on someone in my presence.

You, O Lord, Gave Me

I was wandering in life, for I had no hope, no focus and no dreams. I was like a sinking boat.

I wandered through my life, not knowing who I was or where I was going.

The Lord showed His mercy on me, called me into His flock and gave me all that I needed to be His child.

You, O Lord, gave me hope and let me smile, even when I am feeling down.

You, O Lord, gave me focus on Your holy ground, so I know that Your love is all around me.

You, O Lord, gave me a dream beyond my wandering life that had no beams of light.

You, O Lord, gave me a water stream of your forgiveness and goodness leading me to repent.

Some Who Know Me

Some who know me and believed that I would not prosper beyond my failures were so right, until my Lord proved them wrong.

After the Lord stepped in, none of their words were true about me.

I was doomed to be like the dirt on the ground being walked all over by their opinion of me, until Jesus Christ, my Lord, planted his seeds of mercy and grace down in the spiritual dirt of my soul.

I decided to make Jesus my bright sunshine and rain showers, and I decided to love and obey Jesus.

In the eyes of all who know me to have failed and be nothing in life, my bad choices made me look like a fool.

My Lord Jesus proved I was no fool, and He set me free from my failures.

Some who know me believed I'm not supposed to be blessed by the Lord.

The Lord will not deceive me, leave me or forsake me.

My trials are as high as a mountain, for my life too look so scared up in the eyes of who know me only by outward appearance.

My Lord Jesus brought me safely through it all, and now they are shocked.

From My Heart

I am trying my best to write prose poetry from my heart to share with you.

I want to be real with you in my prose poetry that I love to write.

I try my best to write what I feel.

I try my best to write what I see.

I try my best to write what I experienced.

I try my best to write the truth.

Whatever prose poem The Lord inspires me to write, I must share it with others, so they can be blessed by my poetry.

I believe by faith that some people will be blessed by my inspiring prose poetry.

I believe that some people can relate to my prose poetry.

I love to write prose poetry from my heart because I want to be real with others, whether they are blessed or not blessed by what I write.

I believe by faith that the Lord inspires me to write prose poetry so that I can help myself keep my faith in Him.

I believe by faith that the Lord inspires me to write prose poetry to help others keep their faith in him.

Whatever poem The Lord inspires me to write, I know that I must write it.

Some prose poems the Lord inspires me to write are easy to write.

Some prose poems the Lord inspires me to write are hard to write.

Some prose poems the Lord inspires me to write are ones I don't want to write.

I believe by faith that the Lord gives me good prose poems to write and share with others whether they like it or not after they read my prose poetry.

My prose poetry is from my heart and I need the Lord to make it real.

I want my prose poetry to be real and true from my heart.

If you read my prose poetry, I pray and hope that you will understand what I feel, what I see and what I experienced to share with you.

I am sharing with you my faith in the Lord.

I am sharing with you my relationship with the Lord.

I am sharing with you my testimonies about the Lord.

I am sharing with you my hope in the Lord.

I am sharing with you my love for the Lord.

I am sharing with you that I know that I need the Lord in my life.

I wouldn't want to write prose poetry if I couldn't write it from my heart.

Some people may like my prose poetry and some people may not like my prose poetry, even though the Lord inspired me to write it to help others to see the truth.

My prose poetry helps me to see the truth about myself and I believe that it will help other people to see the truth about themselves.

The Lord Jesus Christ, who I believe in, is the Living Truth and he surely knows how to show you and me the truth about ourselves.

The Lord has shown me a lot of truth about myself in the prose poems that he has inspired me to write.

If you read my prose poetry, you will have a good idea about who I am in the Lord.

The Lord has brought me a long way and I know that I still have a long way to go in the Lord.

On my Christian journey that is not easy, I want to share my prose poetry about my Lord with you so that you can read and hopefully understand my walk with the Lord even though it may be different from your walk with the Lord.

Prose poetry from my heart is what I love to share with others who I want to be real with.

I worship a real Lord and Savior who is always real with you and me.

You and I don't have to be educated to be real.

I can only be me and you can only be you, but I hope that the prose poetry that I write will influence you to not judge me if it is not up on your spiritual level.

My prose poetry about the Lord is plain and simple, for me to be who I am from my heart.

I can only give you my realness, I know that you will either accept it or not accept it.

The most important thing to me is that the Lord accepts me being real in my prose poetry that is never worthless to him, even if some people don't like my prose poetry.

I am learning so much that everyone will not be blessed by what you and I do for the Lord.

I am very thankful unto the Lord that there are some people who are blessed by my prose poetry about the Lord.

My prose poetry is not about causing anyone to feel good when you read it.

My prose poetry is about causing you and me to be convicted of our sins.

No one feels good about being convicted of the wrongs that we do.

I love writing serious prose poetry because we are living in serious times and I know Jesus Christ is coming back again.

Jesus is serious about saving you and me from our sins.

Feel-good poetry may be for those who are not real with themselves about accepting the truth of needing to be convicted and converted by the Holy Spirit.

All of my prose poetry is spiritual from the Holy Spirit who reveals to us the whole truth.

Some of my prose poetry steps on my toes to convict me of my sins.

I don't want to share prose poetry with you if it doesn't do anything good for me.

Pastors can preach sermons and bible school teachers can spread the Gospel of Jesus Christ.

But if the pastor's sermon doesn't do the pastor any good then why would the pastor want their sermons to do you and me any good?

It's the same thing with my poetry.

My prose poetry about the Lord does me good and I believe that it will do some other people good too.

The Lord hasn't failed me yet in my prose poetry.

To God be the glory.

That Split Second Between Life and Death

On a weekday in the early afternoon, I left my house and got in my car.

My mind was on going to the T-Mobile store to get my phone back in service.

I also had my mind on getting my second covid-19 vaccine shot.

When I got in my car, I drove out of my parking space and entered onto the main road that leads to the upcoming traffic.

I stopped at the end of the road where I was supposed to wait until the traffic was clear.

I was a little impatient when a trash truck driver slowed down to turn off the road.

The trash truck driver drove close to me as I was on the opposite side of the main road that leads out.

Before the trash truck driver made his turn off of the road, I began to drive in front of him because I didn't see the oncoming traffic.

I truly thank the Lord that I drove out slowly and was able to quickly press down on the brakes to stop just in time before a speeding vehicle could hit me.

I believe that the Lord must have sent down an angel from heaven to force my feet down onto the brake pedal at the right time.

That angel came from Heaven a lot faster than the speed of light because it was just a split second between life and death that I was able to hit my brakes.

I didn't have time to think about hitting my break.

It was a miracle to me that my foot pressed down on the brake pedal really fast.

That very moment was like my life was moving in slow motion and that vehicle was moving fast, ready to hit my car and probably kill me.

The Lord showed me that it wasn't my time to leave here and join the dead.

The Lord showed me that no matter what good things I do, it's not enough to prolong my life if it's my time to join the dead.

The Lord showed me that he is the one who can truly shorten my life or prolong my life.

I am so happy that the Lord spared my life in that split second between life and death.

I am so glad that the Lord is not finished with me yet.

The devil wanted me to be hit by that speeding vehicle that I couldn't see because of the trash truck blocking the view.

If I had been in a big hurry to drive around the trash truck, I probably would have been killed.

The Lord was surely ahead of me to see that speeding vehicle that I didn't see coming my way.

The Lord sent down an angel from Heaven to force my foot down on the brake pedal in the split second between life and death.

The Lord showed me that everything is about His time and not my time.

I can make my time be short and surely not know when the Lord has the power to rule over my time and give me more time to live beyond a split-second between life and death.

I can easily take my life for granted when the Lord is so merciful and sees fit for me to live through this day that I don't deserve to see.

A split second between life and death can be a frightening experience, and if the Lord is in it, there will be a calmness in our spirit that the devil can't disturb.

Having Faith in You, O Lord

Having faith in You, O Lord, keeps me going strong.

Having faith in You, O Lord, helps me to live in reality.

Having faith in You, O Lord, help me to do your holy will.

Having faith in You, O Lord, helps me to love everybody.

Having faith in You, O Lord, gives me something good to look forward to.

Having faith in You, O Lord, is the best thing in my life.

Having faith in You, O Lord, help me to keep my eyes on you.

Having faith in You, O Lord, makes me strong when I am weak.

Having faith in You, O Lord, helps me to love you and keep your Commandments.

Having faith in You, O Lord, gives me encouragement.

Having faith in You, O Lord, motivates me to live right.

Having faith in You, O Lord, helps me to be honest with everybody.

Having faith in You, O Lord, lifts me up when I am feeling down

Having faith in You, O Lord, helps me to meditate on you.

Having faith in You, O Lord, helps me to read your holy word.

Having faith in You, O Lord, brings me back to You when I am feeling lost.

Having faith in You, O Lord, helps me to think on spiritual things.

Having faith in You, O Lord, helps me to walk on Your straight and narrow road.

Having faith in You, O Lord, helps me to face up to my trials.

Having faith in You, O Lord, helps me to finish what I started.

Having faith in You, O Lord, helps me to not be too hard on myself.

Having faith in You, O Lord, helps me to not be hard on others.

Having faith in You, O Lord, gives me hope in this sinful world.

Having faith in You, O Lord, helps me to know that I have a lot to live for.

Having faith in You, O Lord, helps me to stay awake spiritually to be ready for Your second coming back to this world.

I See You

My Lord Jesus Christ, I see You telling me the truth in Your holy word that I must read for myself.

Oh, my Lord, I see you opening up my blind spiritual eyes so that I can see You are the living truth.

My Lord Jesus Christ, I see You telling me to pray without ceasing in Your holy word.

I know that whenever I pray to You, You will lift me up from the pits of stress and cause me to feel a lot better so my mind can shine in Your glory.

My Lord Jesus Christ, I see You talking to me in Your holy word and counseling me to deny myself, pick up my cross and follow you one day at a time.

I see you, my Lord Jesus Christ, talking to me so kindly with authority.

You get through to me so I can see that You love me and will save my soul for believing in You.

My Lord Jesus Christ, I see you quenching my thirsty soul in Your holy word that lets me know that You are the living waters of life that I can drink and You will refresh my soul.

Oh, my Lord and Savior Jesus Christ, I see you feeding my hungry soul with your holy word that lets me know that you are the bread of life that will never get stale and will never mold.

Only you, my Lord Jesus, can fill up my hungry soul with the truth and set me free from spiritual starvation.

Oh, my Lord, I see You encouraging me to hold on to You and Your holy word because You are the word of God and the word was made flesh and lived among sinners like me.

My Lord Jesus Christ, I see You in Your holy word from the book of Genesis to the book of Revelations where all the prophets of God and all the disciples point to You to fulfill their existence and divine missions from You.

My Lord Jesus Christ, I see You giving me spiritual strength, mental strength and the physical strength to make it through the day.

Your holy word backs me up, because You are Your holy word that fills up my life with hope and faith in You from day to day.

Oh, my Lord Jesus Christ, I see You telling me to love You and obey You in Your holy word that You fulfilled before You created the heavens and the earth.

Oh Lord, You Always Know

Oh Lord, You always know me better than I will ever know myself.

Oh Lord, You always know what is good and not good for me.

Oh Lord, You always know what I can bear and what I can't bear.

Oh Lord, You always know whose life to shorten and you always know whose life to prolong.

Oh Lord, You always know all that I don't know.

Oh Lord, You always know all who hate me.

Oh Lord, You always know all who love me.

Oh Lord, You always know who talks bad about me.

Oh Lord, You always know all of my thoughts.

Oh Lord, You always know what I will say before I say it.

Oh Lord, You always know what I will do before I do it.

Oh Lord, You always know what I will dream before I dream it.

Oh Lord, You always know what I will see before I see it.

Oh Lord, You always know what I will hear before I hear it.

Oh Lord, You always know what I will feel before I feel it.

Oh Lord, You always know everything that I do.

Oh Lord, You always know everything that I feel.

Oh Lord, You always know all of my mind.

Old Lord, You are you always know all of my heart.

Oh Lord, You always do all of my life.

Oh Lord, You always know what choices I will make.

Old Lord, You always know all the right things that I do.

Oh Lord, You always know all the wrong things that I do.

Oh Lord, You always know all of my sins.

Oh Lord, You always know all of my weaknesses.

Oh Lord, You always know what I know.

Oh Lord, You always know all of my sins.

Oh Lord, You always know all of my disappointments.

Oh Lord, You always know all of my sorrow.

Oh Lord, You always know my joy.

Oh Lord, You always know all of my pain.

Oh Lord, You always know my destiny.

Oh Lord, You always know me every day.

Oh Lord, You always know everybody's mind, heart and soul.

Oh Lord, You always know everybody's choices and whether they choose You or reject You.

Doing Your Holy Will, O Lord

Doing Your holy will, O Lord, is so good for my Soul.

Doing Your holy will, O Lord, is so glorious.

Doing Your holy will, O Lord, is so magnificent.

Doing Your holy will, O Lord, is so very rewarding.

Doing Your holy will, O Lord, is more beautiful than any woman in this world.

Doing Your holy will, O Lord, is victorious.

Doing Your holy will, O Lord, is so great to me.

Doing Your holy will, O Lord is so vibrant to me.

Doing Your holy will, O Lord is the best thing in my life.

Doing Your holy will, O Lord, gives me the strength to keep going on.

Doing Your holy will, O Lord, gives me peace of mind.

Doing Your holy will, O Lord, lifts me up on a spiritual high.

Doing Your holy will, O Lord, is every good thing to me.

Doing Your holy will, O Lord, gives me hope from day to day.

Doing Your holy will, O Lord, gives me mental powers.

Doing Your holy will, O Lord, makes me happy.

Doing Your holy will, O Lord, help me to love everybody.

Doing Your holy will, O Lord, encourages me to love you more and more.

Doing Your holy will, O Lord, is 24 hours, around the clock.

Doing Your holy will, O Lord, is stronger than any man in this world.

Doing Your holy will, O Lord, is higher than the highest mountain.

Doing Your holy will, O Lord, is more beautiful than the lily in the valley.

Doing Your holy will, O Lord, shines brighter than the sun.

Doing Your holy will, O Lord, is from everlasting to everlasting.

Doing Your holy will, O Lord, is everything that I need.

Doing Your holy will, O Lord, is better than anything in this world.

Doing Your holy will, O Lord, protects me from doing my will.

Doing Your holy will, O Lord, gives me the strength to get through the day.

Doing Your holy will, O Lord, is the best thing that can happen in my life.

Doing Your holy will, O Lord, causes death to move farther away from me.

Doing Your holy will, O Lord, is never a lost cause to me or anyone else.

Doing Your holy will, O Lord, is not only for me to do on earth but also for me to do in heaven too.

Doing Your holy will, O Lord, lets my enemies see that You, O Lord, are for me and not against me.

Doing Your holy will, O Lord, helps me to make this world a better place to live in.

Oh Lord, You Know

Oh Lord, You know what to allow me to go through to mold me and shape me into being faithful unto You.

Oh Lord, You know what to allow me to go through to help me to be obedient unto You.

Oh Lord, You know what to allow me to go through to help me to be humble unto You.

Oh Lord, You know what to allow me to go through to help me to hold onto You.

Oh Lord, you know what to allow me to go through to help me keep my eyes on You.

Oh Lord, you know me so much better than I will ever know myself.

Oh Lord, you know me so much better and anyone else will ever know me.

Oh Lord, you know where I have been and You know where I'm going.

Oh Lord, you know all of my thoughts.

Oh Lord, You know all of my mind.

Oh Lord, You know all of my words.

Oh Lord, You know all of my actions.

Oh Lord, you know all of my heart.

Oh Lord, I will never know myself like You know me.

Oh Lord, no one else will ever know me like You know me.

Oh Lord, You know all of my mistakes.

Oh Lord, You know all of my flaws.

Oh Lord, You know all of my failures.

Oh Lord, You know all of my rejections.

Oh Lord, You know all of my fears.

Oh Lord, You know all of my heartaches.

Oh Lord, You know all of my grief.

Old Lord, You know me all of my life-long days.

Oh Lord, You know all of the ups and downs in my life.

Oh Lord, You know all of my weaknesses.

Oh Lord, You know all my sins.

Oh Lord, You know all of my burdens.

Oh Lord, You know all of my works.

Oh Lord, You know all of my motives.

Oh Lord, You know all of my intentions.

Oh Lord, there is nothing that You don't know.

Oh Lord, You know what I will think before I think it.

Oh Lord, You know what I will say before I say it.

Oh Lord, You know what I will do before I do it.

Oh Lord, You know all of my pain.

Oh Lord, You know all of my joy.

Oh Lord, You know all of my victories.

Oh Lord, You know all of me, inside and out.

Oh Lord, You know all of my past.

Oh Lord, You know all of my present.

Oh Lord, You know all of my future.

Oh Lord, You know my destiny so much more than I will ever know and so much more than anyone else will ever know.

Be in My

Be in my mind, O Lord, for me to think on You day after day.

Be in my heart, O Lord, for me to always love You.

Be in my eyes, O Lord, for me to see Your mercy.

Be in my ears, O Lord, for me to hear Your holy word.

Be in my mouth, O Lord, for me to speak Your holy word in love.

Be in my hands, O Lord, for me to open my bible and study it.

Be in my arms, O Lord, for me to wrap my arms around hurting people in the church and outside the church.

Be in my legs, O Lord, for me to stand on Your promises.

Be in my motives, O Lord, for me to have good reasons.

Be in my intentions, O Lord, for me to do the right things.

Be in my health, O Lord, for me to eat right and exercise my body that is Your temple to dwell in.

Be in my home, O Lord, for me to be Your church in my home.

Be in my vehicle, O Lord, for me to drive safe on the road and to respect other drivers.

Be in my comings and goings, O Lord, for me to represent You wherever I go here and there.

Be in my life, O Lord, for me to live right by example before the world every day that You, O Lord, are a righteous and holy Lord and Savior.

Be in my destiny, O Lord, for me to be saved in You and go with You to heaven when You come back again.

Be in my existence, O Lord, for me to have stars on my crown for winning souls to make it to heaven because You, O Lord, allowed me to still exist today in this world where I can choose to live for You and be a witness of You before others.

Nobody Can Tell Me

Nobody can tell me that God is not good.

Nobody can tell me that God is not kind.

Nobody can tell me that God is not merciful.

Nobody can tell me that God is not miraculous.

Nobody can tell me that God is not a second chance God.

Nobody can tell me that God is not love.

God loves every human being and God loves all animals.

Nobody can tell me that God is not victorious.

The Lord God has blessed me with two little dogs, one is a boy and the other is a girl.

I give them their dog medicine every morning to ease their itching paws and ears.

When I give them their medicine in the form of a pill, I wrap the pill in a turkey slice.

They love the meat so much that they don't spit out the pill.

One morning when I gave my boy dog his medicine, I was a little distracted by the girl dog walking past me.

When I gave the boy dog his medicine, I always use a corn prong holder that I hold tight in my hand.

I use that because my boy dog will bite my fingers trying to get that turkey meat.

That morning when I was distracted, I wasn't holding the corn prong holder tightly enough and when my boy dog leaped up to eat the turkey he pulled the meat and the corn prong holder out of my hand and almost swallowed it.

I was so frightened that he would die if he swallowed that.

It seemed like everything was happening in slow motion and I couldn't do anything to stop him.

I truly know that God intervened right on time and kept my little boy dog from swallowing that corn prong holder that probably would have killed him.

Nobody can tell me that God is not an on-time God who spared my dog from suffering and possible death.

God has spared me from suffering because God didn't allow my dog to die when I was helpless and frozen in my tracks.

God also loves the animals that He created for His pleasure.

God the Father, the Son, and the Holy Spirit showed me a different way to give my little boy dog his medicine after that frightening day.

I realize the Lord had been merciful to me all the times before this when I'd been giving my dogs their medicine.

I truly believe God had been trying to tell me not to use the corn prong holder, but I didn't listen to God.

Thankfully, God is a loving and merciful God who gives us even more than a second chance to get things right before it's too late.

I Believe in Jesus Christ

I believe in Jesus Christ because His goodness to me has led me to confess and repent of my sins.

I believe in Jesus Christ because Jesus has given me more than one chance to live my life unto Him.

I believe in Jesus Christ because Jesus has spared my life from death many times so I could live to see this day.

I believe in Jesus Christ because Jesus didn't give up on me when I had given up on myself.

I believe in Jesus Christ because Jesus is always there for me on my good days and bad days.

I believe in Jesus Christ because Jesus has shown me that He cannot fail me.

I believe in Jesus Christ because Jesus brought me through hardships that no one else could bring me through.

I believe in Jesus Christ because Jesus never turned His back on me even when I had turned my back on Him.

I believe in Jesus Christ because Jesus is always faithful and true to me.

I believe in Jesus Christ because Jesus winked his eye at my ignorance when I didn't know the truth of His holy word.

I believe in Jesus Christ because Jesus never looked down on me with condemnation when I was living in darkness.

I believe in Jesus Christ because Jesus is my best friend every day, and I can talk to Jesus about anything and He will understand.

I believe in Jesus Christ because Jesus is worthy to be praised every day that no one else can do what Jesus can do for me.

I believe in Jesus Christ because Jesus is all-powerful in my life and I live safely in His protection that cannot fail me like luck has failed me many times.

I believe in Jesus Christ because I know that it's Jesus who blesses my mind with the right thoughts so that I can write them down in words about Him to share with others in published books of prose poetry about Him.

I believe in Jesus Christ because Jesus has never forsaken me when I needed Him most.

I believe in Jesus Christ because I know that Jesus has forgiven me of all my past sins.

I believe in Jesus Christ because Jesus didn't turn me down when I decided to give my life to Him after I was all broken down in the devil's lies that I was living.

I believe in Jesus Christ because I know that Jesus has brought me this far in life even though I don't deserve it.

I believe in Jesus Christ because Jesus spiritually operated on my heart and cut out that old sinful me and cleaned me up spiritually to love Him and keep His Commandments in my heart.

I believe in Jesus Christ because Jesus is always on time to answer my prayers, even when I doubt that He hears me.

I believe in Jesus Christ because I know that Jesus loves me the same as He loves everybody else in this world.

I believe in Jesus Christ because Jesus didn't let the devil destroy me when I was living in my sins.

I believe in Jesus Christ because Jesus is the only true One who I can believe in, because no human being on earth can give me eternal life.

I believe in Jesus Christ because I know that only Jesus is worthy to be worshipped above idol gods that can't make a way out of a no way death threat situation.

I believe in Jesus Christ because Jesus has kept me safe from my old sinful self who once tried to take my own life but Jesus stepped in and spared my life so I could live to see this day.

Jesus has the last decision to make that is always right and fair for my life.

I believe in Jesus Christ because Jesus has proven to me that if I was the only sinner living among perfect people who could do everything right, He would give up his life just to save me from my sins to make me perfect and have no sins so I could do everything perfect.

I believe in Jesus Christ because Jesus has opened doors for me that nobody can shut.

I believe in Jesus Christ because Jesus has shown His great mercy on me.

I believe in Jesus Christ because Jesus has helped me to wise up and not do foolish things anymore.

I believe in Jesus Christ because Jesus has shown me that there is nothing too hard for Him to work things out in my life.

I believe in Jesus Christ because Jesus has shown me that He is the healer of ill motives, ill intentions and ill feelings that man-made medicines can't heal.

I believe in Jesus Christ because He so loved me first, when I didn't love myself.

I believe in Jesus Christ because I know that Jesus didn't bring me this far to let me down.

I believe in Jesus Christ because there is no one else who is worthy to believe in above Jesus, who is the Son of God.

I believe in Jesus Christ because Jesus has done things for me and is doing things for me today that no one else can do for me.

I believe in Jesus Christ because I know today, without a doubt, that Jesus kept death from taking me to the grave that I deserved a long time ago and up until this day that Jesus gives the final say-so over life and death that the devil can't override regardless of so many lives that he has already taken to the grave.

I believe in Jesus Christ because I truly know today that Jesus always knows what is best for me and He will save me from being lost in my sins.

No one else will always know what is best for me and will keep me from doing things that will cause me more harm than good.

I believe in Jesus Christ because Jesus has always been truthful with me and has never deceived me, even though at one time I deceived myself and believed that I didn't need Jesus in my life.

I Look at Myself in the Mirror

I look at myself in the mirror and I see God's love upon me, who wouldn't know what love is without loving God.

I look at myself in the mirror and I see God's mercy upon me, who is alive today because of God's mercy.

I look at myself in the mirror and I see God's grace upon me, who is in my right mind today because of God's grace.

I look at myself in the mirror and I see God's forgiveness upon me, who knows what it means to forgive myself and others because of God's forgiveness.

I look at myself in the mirror and I see God's long-suffering upon me, who must suffer in denying self and picking up my cross to follow Jesus because of God's long-suffering.

I look at myself in the mirror and I see God's goodness upon me, who is a Christian today because of God's goodness.

I look at myself in the mirror and I see God's healing upon me, who is spiritually healed by the truth of God's holy word because of God's healing power.

I look at myself in the mirror and I see God's protection upon me in my house and wherever I go and come back home safely because of God's protection.

I look at myself in the mirror and I see God's peace upon me, who lives in a troublesome world with a peace of mind because of God's peace.

I look at myself in the mirror and I see God's Holy Spirit upon me, who can love even my enemies and hope that they will believe in Jesus Christ and be saved before it's too late.

I look at myself in the mirror and I see God's salvation upon me, who loves to pray to Jesus and live for Jesus because I love Jesus who gave up His life on the cross to save me from my sins.

I look at myself in the mirror and I see the devil who doesn't want me to see that it's God who is so good to me all the time.

I look at myself in the mirror and I see the devil who doesn't want me to see that it's God who brought me this far in my life because the devil wants me to look at myself in the mirror and believe that I brought myself this far in my life.

I see God with me when I look at myself in the mirror, and I truly know that I am saved in God's Son, Jesus Christ.

I look at myself in the mirror and I see God's strength upon me to keep me mentally, emotionally, physically and spiritually strong in my difficult experiences in life.

I look at myself in the mirror and I see God is with me, and I know that the devil can't deceive me into believing that God is not for me, even though my enemies are against me.

When I look at myself in the mirror, the devil wants me to see only me giving myself the glory and praise for what God is doing for me in my life.

When I look at myself in the mirror, the devil wants me to see only me being caught up in myself, who God kept safe in my mother's womb.

Today, I can look at myself in the mirror and I see that God has given me a second chance to love Him and keep His Commandments; that is God's character.

Today, I can look at myself in the mirror and I see that God didn't leave me all alone when I was living in darkness that would have killed me if God had allowed it.

Today, I can look at myself in the mirror and I see that God is with me, because God has opened my spiritual blind eyes to look into His mirror of Commandments that have no spots or stains on them, when man-made mirrors can get spots and stains on them and not let me see myself clearly.

I look at myself in the mirror and I see no good thing in me without Jesus Christ being in my heart to help me to be good to myself and my neighbors.

I look at myself in the mirror and I see a lost soul if I don't confess and repent of my sins unto the Lord.

If I hold onto even one sin and don't confess and repent of that sin unto Jesus, I will be lost.

I was Young and Foolish

I grew up without a father in the home.

During my high school years, I played a lot of hooky from going to school.

I would leave out of the house and pretend that I was going to school, but then I would hide behind the house until my mother went to work.

After my mother left out of the house, I would go back in the house and watch TV.

I would also bake buttered bread in the oven and cook some eggs on the stove.

I played hooky from school and don't even know why I did it.

When I did go to school, no one asked me where I had been.

I also don't remember my mother ever looking at my report cards to see my grade and my attendance in school.

I don't know how I was able to pass my classes in high school.

I passed from the ninth grade to the tenth grade and from the eleventh grade to the twelfth grade with a C grade point average.

If I had taken going to school seriously, I believe that my grades would have been much higher.

I was young and foolish, because when I did go to school I would hang around with bad company and drink wine after school was over.

I believed that I was having a good time, but I didn't see how foolish I was.

I deceived my mother when I made her believe that I was going to school, but most of all I deceived myself and robbed myself of the opportunity to do my best in school.

I was young and foolish, but there were many other young and wise high school students who graduated with a high grade point average and went on to college.

I feel regret today because I did not take going to school seriously, but the Lord showed mercy on me and allowed me to be doing as well as I am today.

I was young and foolish and didn't know it, but I know today that I am serious about living my life unto the Lord Jesus Christ.

The Lord has helped me to wise up so that I know that education is for life, especially getting educated about God's holy word that is full of wisdom to get the foolishness out of anyone.

For a Long Time

The devil has been trying to destroy me for a long time, because he knew that when I gave my life unto the Lord there would be no turning back to him.

The devil has tried to destroy me since I was a little child, like when I was sexually assaulted.

The devil tried to destroy me when I was a little boy who was trapped in the trunk of an old car. The devil tried to destroy me when I was a teenager who drank alcohol and smoked cigarettes.

The devil tried his best to destroy me.

The Lord didn't let the devil destroy me because the Lord knew that I would one day give my life unto Him.

The devil tried to destroy me in my young adult years when I used drugs that caused me to have a nervous breakdown that lasted the rest of my young adult years.

God knew that the devil didn't want me to live to see the day where I truly know that the Lord God, Jesus Christ brought me this far.

Jesus Christ has brought me this far so that I can love and obey Him day after day.

For a long time, the devil tried to destroy me because he knew that I would give my life to the Lord, and give my Lord Jesus Christ my best, regardless of what I went through in my life.

The devil tried to destroy me for a long time.

He tried to destroy me when a group of young men beat me up at a party that I wasn't invited to.

The devil tried to destroy me when a drunken man put a gun to my head.

The devil tried to destroy me when my manic depressive first wife put a knife to my throat while I was driving her to the naval hospital for a biopsy.

She died from breast cancer some months later because she refused to get chemotherapy treatments.

The Lord God Jesus Christ didn't let her kill me when she put that knife to my throat.

The devil tried to destroy me when I went to jail.

My manic depressive first wife was abusive towards me and I tried to defend myself and get away from her, but she followed behind me when I ran outside the apartment and I was arrested because some neighbor called the police.

The Lord didn't let the devil destroy me in jail where I was locked up for four months.

The devil tried to destroy me when I fell asleep while driving my car home from work.

The Lord woke me up in a matter of a few seconds, and I was shocked to see that I was right beside a tractor trailer truck that I could have swerved into.

God didn't let the devil destroy me because God knew that when I gave my life unto Him I would give testimonies about what He brought me through.

God has been with me for a long time, and the devil hates that because God didn't let him destroy me, which means I get to see this day that I know I truly don't deserve to be alive.

The devil tried to destroy me when I was having a sexual relationship with some married women.

I had a sexual relationship with one of the women in her husband's house, and the Lord showed mercy on me and didn't let her husband walk in on us.

The devil tried to destroy me when I got involved in a deadly quarrel between a man and a woman one night.

The man was very mad at his girlfriend and left the house.

He ran down the street and came back with a long metal pipe in his hand, which I saw when I left out of the house.

I looked to see where he went, and I saw him running very fast toward me with the long metal pipe in his hand as I held a long knife in my hand.

I know today that the Lord stopped him in his tracks to keep him from hitting me with that metal pipe, which could have killed me.

The devil tried to destroy me a long time ago, but the Lord spared my life even through all of my ignorance and mistakes that the devil used to try to destroy me.

There were other things that happened in my life that the devil used to try to destroy me too, but the Lord Almighty protected my life and kept me from death and the early grave that I deserved when the Lord knew that I would be a new creature in Him today.

The devil tried to destroy me a long time ago when I was an 18-year-old virgin who joined the military and then had sex with a prostitute.

The Lord showed mercy on me and didn't allow me to get a deadly venereal disease.

My Lord God and Savior Jesus Christ didn't let the devil destroy me in my rebellion against Him.

The devil tried to destroy me simply because I exist and have the opportunity to be saved in Jesus Christ and make it to heaven where the devil once lived but got kicked out of.

The devil tried to destroy me in my sins because he didn't want me to exist today to live for the Lord.

God gave the devil a chance to repent up in heaven, but the devil's chances had run out.

The Lord didn't let the devil destroy me in my sins, because the Lord knew that He could use me because He foresaw me confessing and repenting of my sins and denying myself and picking up my cross to follow Him.

The devil hated to see that happen because he knew that my soul would be anchored in the Lord and there would be no turning back to my past life that the devil had tried to destroy a long time ago when the Lord overthrew his attempts.

I know that there were many other people who are not here in the land of the living today and I don't know the reason why they didn't make it this far.

I know that I can't question God about that because God always knows what He is doing and what He must do for the good of everyone.

The devil tried to destroy everyone a long time ago, and God allowed him to succeed in destroying many people.

I know that I am no better than those people who the devil destroyed a long time ago.

I don't completely know why the Lord God Jesus Christ spared my life and let me see this day that many people had hoped to see.

The devil tried his best to destroy me a long time ago, but the Lord God Jesus Christ looked down on me from heaven and saw something in me that got His attention and He did not let the devil destroy me.

I believe that if I was the only sinner in a world of perfect people, the Lord would have given up His life for me to be saved and make it to Heaven.

God has given me the opportunity to know this today, and I realize He can give a long life to anyone who He chooses and no one can question Him about it.

The devil tried to destroy me a long time ago, and the devil made accusations against me that were true for me to not deserve to be here today, but the Lord confused the devil by lengthening my days so I could see this day of living my life unto the Him.

The devil tried to destroy me when I tried to take my own life by taking an overdose of sleeping pills.

The Lord used my girlfriend to save my life.

I woke up in the hospital the next day.

God didn't let the devil destroy me a long time ago when I was weak-minded and would fall for just about anything the devil tempted me with.

I am so glad today that the Lord didn't give up on me, even when I had given up on myself.

I am happy to give this testimony today about what the Lord brought me through when no one else could bring me through my failures and misfortunes.

God didn't let the devil get the victory over me, and my life was not cut short from the land of the living.

I was spiritually blind a long time ago, but thanks to the Lord, today I see that my soul was never worthless to God who did not let the devil destroy me a long time ago.

That long time ago is like a split second to God, but all it takes is a split second to die in a car accident.

To God, my past life flashed by like a car light flashing by a tree in the night.

God didn't let the devil destroy me a long time ago.

Even though my death might have flashed by many times, God spared my life even when I didn't deserve it.

The devil tried to destroy me a long time ago when I smoked marijuana, smoked hash, used LSD and smoked crack cocaine.

My God, Lord and Savior Jesus Christ didn't let the devil destroy me through those drugs.

I am so glad that the Lord is not finished with me so that I can give my testimonies about all the terrible things that He brought me through.

That old devil didn't want me to live to see this day where I can share with the world that God cannot fail to let you and me live a long life even though the devil sets many death traps for us.

A long time ago, God didn't let the devil destroy me in my sins, and since I gave my life to Him, the Lord has cleansed me from doing those bad things that I did a long time ago.

Today I am a new creature in my Lord and Savior Jesus Christ.

That old sinful me was gone the second I gave my life to Jesus Christ.

The devil tried to destroy me a long time ago, when I was an unarmed security officer who was picking up something at a convenience store.

While I was there, a black man approached me, got all up in my face to start a fight with me.

There were four other black men with him and one of them said, "Let's go," to the man who wanted to start a fight with me.

I know today that it was the Lord who protected me.

That man could have shot me with the gun if the other man hadn't said, "Let's go."

The Lord God didn't let the devil take my life a long time ago.

The devil tried to destroy me a long time ago when I was walking through a violent apartment complex one day and a young man and boy approached me.

They stopped me in my tracks and asked, "What's up, man?"

I said, "The Lord is my redeemer."

There was another man who laughed and said. "Homeboy's mind is gone."

So, the young black man and young boy moved away from me and let me go where I was going.

The Lord protected me that night a long time ago.

The Lord God didn't let the devil destroy me a long time ago.

It's a miracle to me to see this day where I can give my testimonies about what the Lord brought me through.

The devil tried to destroy me when I got circumcised at the age of 14 years old.

I was in so much pain for the whole summer months.

I couldn't do much of anything at all.

My mother had to comfort me when I felt like I would die from the terrible pain.

The Lord didn't let the devil destroy me a long time ago when I was a teenage boy.

The Lord has blessed me to be 64 years old today, and I can look back on my life and know that I didn't bring myself through my hardships — the Lord brought me safely through when I should have died a long time ago.

The Lord showed me that it wasn't my time to die a long time ago because the Lord wasn't finished with me, so He let me live to see this day.

The devil tried to destroy me a long time ago, but he failed and didn't follow through on his plans to kill me.

The Lord foreknew that I would choose to live my life unto Him today.

Even so, the devil is still trying to destroy me, but God has prolonged my life over death and can add on even more years to my life if it's in His holy will.

The devil tried to destroy me a long time ago when I was a little boy who had a heat stroke from playing too much in the summertime heat.

My body was hot and red all over, and someone said they should call the ambulance to take me to the hospital.

The Lord blessed my body to cool off and I didn't have to go to the hospital.

The Lord didn't let the devil destroy me with that heat stroke.

The devil tried to destroy me a long time ago when I was a little boy and fell down the stairs.

I could've broken my neck but the Lord protected me and I only bruised my arm.

The Lord didn't let the devil destroy me a long time ago.

The devil tried to destroy me a long time ago when I was about 12 years old.

There was a big teenage boy who pushed me around and knocked me down several times.

I could have hit my head on something hard and that could have killed me.

The Lord didn't let the devil destroy me.

The devil tried to destroy me a long time ago when I was a newspaper paper carrier at the age of 13.

Two medium-sized dogs tried to attack me while I was riding my bike.

I fought the two dogs and was able to get away from them.

The Lord didn't let the devil destroy me a long time ago.

The devil tried to destroy me a long time ago when I was walking down the street one day in a neighborhood area and two big dogs saw me and ran towards me.

The dogs stopped when they got very close to me.

The Lord spoke to me and told me to stay calm when the dogs sniffed me.

I stayed calm and then the two dogs walked away from me.

The Lord didn't let the devil destroy me a long time ago.

The devil tried to destroy me a long time ago when I was a teenager.

I went to the beach and got caught up in a rip current and I was unable to get out.

I didn't know how to swim and there was no lifeguard around.

The Lord didn't let the devil destroy me — I truly know that today.

I am still alive today because it was the Lord's will for me to be alive today and give my testimony about the bad things that the Lord brought me through.

Those bad things that happened to me a long time ago is like they never happened because of me living my life unto the Lord today.

That long time ago is like a shadow that passed over the landscape.

That long time ago is like waking up out of a bad dream in the early morning sunlight.

That long time ago in my life is like a feather blown away In the wind.

That long time ago went to where the Lord sent it, and that's a place of no return.

The devil tried to destroy me a long time ago because he knew that the Lord could use me to bless someone's life with my testimonies in praise poetry about my Lord and Savior Jesus Christ.

For a long time is like one second to an eternal God who has given me His divine time that I don't deserve to get my life right with Him before it's too late.

It was never too hard for God to bring me this far in my life.

When the devil tried to destroy me a long time ago, God didn't let the devil succeed when I deserved it.

Like a Little Fish Surrounded by Sharks

I was like a little fish surrounded by sharks when I was in the Army at my permanent duty station, Schofield Barracks in Hawaii.

I was 18 years old and inexperienced compared to a lot of the other older soldiers who were very well experienced in their jobs.

I only had a little experience from basic training, compared to the Vietnam War veterans who were all over the barracks where I lived.

I felt like a little fish surrounded by sharks every day.

At my permanent duty station, I had to run three miles, five days a week.

I had to go to the motor pool with some soldiers in my squad to do mechanic work on the dump trucks and jeeps.

I was no mechanic and didn't know how to do that kind of work, but I was surrounded by other soldiers who worked on those vehicles like it was nothing.

There were other soldiers in my company who could drive dump trucks and jeeps, but I could not drive them and didn't have a driver's license.

There were times when I wondered what I had gotten myself into by deciding to become a combat engineer.

When I signed up for the Army, I really didn't know what I was getting myself into.

I didn't know that I would be like a little fish surrounded by sharks.

I know today that the Lord was with me even though I didn't know it at the time.

It was like the wild west where I was stationed in Hawaii.

I hung out with some wild soldiers and experienced things I had never done when I joined the army.

The Lord was with me and protecting me from this wild-wild west.

I was so inexperienced compared to many of the other soldiers, who were from all walks of life all across the nation — there was even a soldier from the Virgin Islands.

My days in the Army were filled with activities.

During the short time I was in the Army, I turned my back on the Lord.

The Lord used two Christian soldiers to try to bring me back to Him, but I didn't care to come back to the Lord at that time.

I took ill and had to be discharged from the Army.

I was like a little fish surrounded by sharks every day, but the Lord didn't let the sharks attack me and eat me up.

I, however, got bitten by some of them because I was so inexperienced and naive in my new environment.

I truly know today that the Lord didn't leave me all alone in my inexperience.

The Lord carried me through when I was like a little fish surrounded by sharks during my short time in the military.

More than What I Asked Him For

The Lord gave me more than what I asked Him for.

Many years ago, I was discharged from the military with a medical honorable discharge.

I had a nervous breakdown from using some illegal drugs that put me in the hospital for six long months.

The psychiatrist gave me some medicine that caused me to feel numb.

When I took that medicine, I couldn't think about anything at all.

When I took that medicine, I couldn't feel anything at all.

I took the medicine for several years, and I felt nothing that whole time.

Every day was like moving in slow motion to me.

Every day was like a fog in my mind.

Every day was like being in a cold freezer.

The medicine caused me to feel like I was paralyzed every day.

Every day was like a cloudy, rainy day.

Every day was like cold water being poured all over me.

The medicine caused me to feel like I was dead for years and years.

Every day was like time passing by me while I stood still.

Every day was like the sun didn't shine on me.

Every day was like me walking on thin ice.

The medicine caused me to feel like I was trapped in a cage.

Every day was like being locked up in prison.

Every day was like being covered in mud.

One day, I prayed to the Lord to help me cry like other people.

I asked the Lord to help me feel emotional pain like other people.

The Lord spoke to me and said, "I will give you a gold mine of feelings."

The Lord gave me more than what I had asked Him for.

The Lord helped me to stop taking the medicine that made me feel so numb.

That medicine was high in dosage and limited me from doing a lot of things.

Today, I am strong in my mind and stable in my mind because of my Lord and Savior Jesus Christ, who didn't let me stay in my bad condition.

The Lord gave me more than what I asked Him for, even though I didn't think I deserved it.

No one can tell me what the Lord can't do for me, especially since He fixed my broken down mind.

The Lord has truly fixed me up and made me able to write about my past ordeals and share them with others who are not judgmental.

The Lord can give you and me more than what we ask Him for.

He always knows we can use what He gives us to uplift His holy name so we can help others to give God the glory and praise for what He has done for them.

Even After I Got Sick

I was medically honorably discharged from the military, but I still smoked pot and drank alcohol even though I was sick.

I was mentally sick because of smoking some bad marijuana.

After I got sick, I didn't wise up and stop smoking marijuana and drinking beer, wine and liquor.

I smoked marijuana with my girlfriend and drank alcohol like it was a recreation.

I was still sick, but not sick enough to stop what I was doing.

I also smoked marijuana with two of my half-brothers and drank a lot of beer with them too.

I was sick in my mind and at the same time I was able to function normally like everyone else.

Even after I got sick, I was able to still work because my military doctor didn't give me 100% disability.

My military doctor discharged me from the military with a 30% disability, so that I still had to work.

I worked different jobs even though I was sick with the mental condition.

I did normal things just like everyone else.

The people I hung around with didn't treat me like I was sick.

They accepted me for who I was, since I was no trouble to them.

I was sick, but not a troublemaker.

I was sick, but not stupid.

I was sick, but not bad.

My mother knew that I was sick after I was discharged from the military.

My mother knew that I was different from the way I used to be before I got sick, but she didn't change on me just because I was sick mentally.

My mother was good to me and treated me like I wasn't sick.

My step-father and sisters never changed on me either.

They were good to me in my sick condition.

All of my kinfolks were good to me.

They never treated me bad when I was sick mentally.

It didn't even seem like I was sick because they treated me normally.

Even after I got sick, the Lord didn't give up on me.

The Lord foresaw me confessing and repenting of my sins unto Him and living my life unto Him today.

The military doctors had given me life-long medicine to take for my mental sickness.

The Lord gave me the life-long spiritual medicine of His mercy and grace for me to take beyond my mental sickness.

The Lord didn't allow my sickness to get the best of me.

Nature Got Mad

Nature got mad at those two teenaged boys who sexually assaulted me when I was a little boy.

They sexually assaulted me in the backyard outhouse.

They sexually assaulted me more than once.

That terrible, degrading act gave me a dim outlook on life.

I felt so ashamed of myself for many years and I did not tell anyone what happened to me.

This forever changed my life in my early childhood years.

My life had suddenly changed in some dark ways that I did not understand.

Those two teenaged boys had befriended my family, but my family just didn't know what they did to me.

After what happened to me, I wasn't that little happy boy anymore.

As I grew up, I lived my life as if I was never sexually assaulted, and that caused me to wander through life with no real meaning or idea of who I was.

I would get into fights, and just didn't care at all.

When no one knew what had happened to me, nature knew what had happened and got mad at those two teenaged boys.

Nature was my witness when I felt so all alone and so ashamed that I covered it up for years and years.

I would make friends, but I had no real trust and couldn't get close to them.

When I grew up to be a man, I joined the Army and wanted to prove to myself that I could be a man of war and fight in battles.

I never got a chance to do that though, because I got ill from using illegal drugs.

I got well trained in being a combat soldier in basic training.

I was ready to take on anything that came my way, but sadly I wasn't trained to protect myself from those two teenaged boys who sexually assaulted me when I was a little boy.

I don't ever remember crying about what happened to me.

I was so angry that I hid what had happened from my family, because I just didn't know how to express it in a civilized way.

I turned to a promiscuous lifestyle.

I had girlfriends I used for sex.

I had some one-night stands with different women.

I knew that my bad behavior all stemmed from the sexual assault that was done to me.

I was in and out of relationships with the women who came into my life.

I was terribly wounded in my soul and pretended that I was all right and that it was okay to use those women for sex.

This was my way of escaping my pain that was like a leech sucking the blood out of my body.

I also drank alcohol and smoked cigarettes, but that could not heal my pain.

For years and years, I wondered why I was left all alone to be assaulted.

I felt like my life was a dry well.

I felt like my life was broken glass.

I felt like my life was a faded picture in a frame.

I felt like my life was sand running out of an hourglass.

I felt like my life was a toothache.

I felt like my life was a dusty book on a shelf.

I felt like my life was a big hole in the wall.

I felt like my life was garbage.

I felt like my life was a bad accident.

I felt like my life was a big lie.

I felt like my life was nothing.

When I was sexually assaulted, my whole life changed and I felt like the most filthy carpet that anyone could walk on.

That is what I felt like when I was sexually assaulted by those two boys who were brothers.

It was bad enough to get sexually assaulted by one person, but when it was two people at the same time, even nature wept bitterly.

Nature was mad and I was numb and did not understand how I felt after I was sexually assaulted.

Today, I truly thank Jesus Christ that it wasn't worse than what it was.

Since I've given my life to Jesus, He uses my pain to make me strong so that I can encourage others who have been sexually assaulted and let them know it is not their fault.

Jesus has turned my pain into great strength so that I can write this and share it with others so that they can know that their lives are not a dead end.

Those two teenaged boys sinned against God when they did what they did to me.

They also committed a terrible crime that they got away with.

Today, I am at peace with myself and my Lord Jesus Christ who says that vengeance is His.

My hope Is that my sexual abusers have confessed and repented of their sins unto the Lord and turned away from living in darkness.

What they did to me gives me no excuse to live my life in any kind of way against the Lord, who has brought me this far in my right mind so that I can write this to help strengthen others so they can overcome their trauma from being sexually assaulted.

Nature is mad at those two teenaged boys who sexually assaulted me.

But, nature is happy to see me doing as well as I am in Jesus' name.

Nature knew that when I gave my heart to Jesus, my life would change.

The Lord gave me a treasure chest of poetry to write about Him.

Nature knew that when I gave my heart to Jesus, my life would change.

The Lord gave me an overflow of poetry about Him.

Nature got mad, but is smiling today because I gave my myself to Jesus when my trauma from my sexual assault tried to destroy my life.

Those two teenaged boys sexually assaulted my body, but they could not sexually assault my choice and keep me from making Jesus Christ my Savior.

Those two teenaged boys sexually assaulted my body, but they could not sexually assault my heart and keep me from being saved in Jesus Christ today.

Nature got mad, but will never regret that Jesus used my trauma from my sexual assault to fix me up and make me whole so that I can serve others with my life and my ministry of poetry that is not finished until Jesus says that it is finished.

When I was sexually assaulted, that was the root of a lot of my problems in my life.

That angry part of me died when I gave my life to Jesus Christ.

Nature cried out to God in its madness and asked Jesus to keep me safe and see me through this sexual assault.

Many people have been sexually assaulted.

They feel ashamed and they don't want to talk about it or write about it or shared with others and be transparent.

Nature is always transparent and gives you and me real tranquility in a troubled world.

Nature will get mad at people who don't care who they hurt.

Nature is always true to stay in its place and treat you and me right each day.

Nature got mad and didn't sin against God when Nature witnessed me being sexually assaulted.

God is seen in nature and that teaches me how to be transparent, even when bad influences are trying to corrupt my soul.

When Nature saw those corrupt acts of those two teenaged boys sexually assaulting me, Nature got mad.

Nature asked God to keep those corrupt acts from corrupting me so that I would not do to others what was done to me.

I am so thankful to God today that no one can say that I caused nature to get mad at me.

Nature would not ever convince God to be against me.

I thank Jesus Christ, my Lord, for giving me the strength to write about my sexual assault.

I am sharing my past with others who may be able to relate to what I have been through.

I want to let them know that the Lord can use this type of bad experience to strengthen them, just like He strengthened me.

I Had Lost My Mind

It began when I took some leave time from my military duty and went home.

I took my thirty days of leave time to go back home and spend time with my kinfolks and girlfriend.

I surely spent most of my time with my girlfriend, and I smoked some marijuana with her.

I bought some marijuana from a man I knew and trusted.

Before that, I had bought marijuana and had been smoking some at my permanent duty station in Hawaii.

I was smoking some good marijuana in Hawaii.

That marijuana didn't give me any bad side effects, even though I knew that it was wrong for me to smoke it.

The marijuana I bought from the man I knew back in my hometown was some marijuana that was bad to smoke.

I smoked it anyway, and it caused me to feel good, so I shared it with my girlfriend.

During my thirty days of leave time, I was smoking a lot of marijuana.

One day, I felt funny and I had a feeling like I had never had before.

My leave time was finished and it was time for me to pack up and travel back to my permanent duty station in Hawaii.

I was in the 25th Infantry Division at the Schofield barracks.

I was in the 65th Engineer Battalion in the Army.

I was young and proud of being in the Army.

When I got back to the barracks I lived in with the other soldiers, I felt that funny feeling a lot more and it was getting stronger.

I felt like everyone could see right through me and could read my mind.

I began to isolate myself by staying in my room and not going anywhere.

I had no appetite at all and didn't eat anything.

I lost so much weight that I was absent from some of my formations in the squad.

I just didn't know what was going on with me.

My company Commander ordered all the soldiers in the company to go to the Big Island on a mission for one month.

I had to go, regardless of how I felt.

I had never thought about seeing a doctor before going to the Big Island.

When I got to the Big Island, I still felt so strange around the other soldiers but I found the strength to perform my duties.

One weekend, some other soldiers and I got together to go to one of the towns on the Big Island.

When we got there, we met some young native women and smoked marijuana with them and drank some alcohol.

By this time after spending so much time alone, I had lost a lot of my social skills, but I still hung out with them that weekend.

My 30-day mission was completed on the Big Island, and I didn't feel any different from how I felt before I went there.

As I got back to the barracks, I began to isolate myself again.

One day, I was standing out on the balcony in the barracks and one of my soldier friends who was from New York said to me, "You are not the same as you used to be."

He also said that I needed to see a doctor.

I took his advice and put in for sick leave from my duties.

When I visited the doctor, the doctor asked me some questions about how I was feeling.

I told the doctor how I was feeling, and before I knew what was going on, the doctor had admitted me to the hospital and put me on some medication.

I was in the hospital for some months, and my squad leader visited me to see if I was well enough to come back and perform my duty.

That never happened though, because I was transferred to another hospital in Washington, DC.

I didn't realize that I'd had a nervous breakdown and the marijuana I smoked had been the cause.

One of my doctors told me that I would never be able to socialize again.

I know today that it was Jesus Christ who blessed the medicine to help my mind to heal so that I could live a normal life today.

Jesus proved that doctor wrong when he told me that I would never socialized again.

Thanks to Jesus Christ, I can socialize with people again.

I was discharged from the Army with a medical honorable discharge.

Thanks to the Lord, I was still able to work some jobs.

Today, I am living my life unto the Lord, who has blessed me to overcome my drug addiction.

The Lord has blessed me to be able to socialize with people.

The Lord has blessed me to express myself, even in the poetry that I love to write about my Lord Jesus Christ.

My nervous breakdown caused me to have some memory loss.

My memory is not so good, but I am thankful unto the Lord that my memory is as good as it is because I am able to have the knowledge to write poetry about the Lord.

When I lost my mind, the devil meant it for my bad but the Lord used it for my good so I could help encourage others and show them that there is nothing the Lord can't do for them.

I think about King Nebuchadnezzar who lost his mind for seven years.

God restored his mind, even though God had caused him to lose it in the first place because Nebuchadnezzar had wanted people to worship him like he was God.

No matter what caused me to lose my mind, I am so glad that the Lord God has restored my mind.

I know that I don't deserve this because I was living in sin against God, who showed me His mercy.

Thanks to Jesus Christ, today the devil doesn't make me smoke marijuana and use illegal drugs anymore.

No human being made me smoke that marijuana and use illegal drugs.

I am to blame, and today I own up to it because the Lord showed me that I must answer to Him alone.

Whether I caused myself to have a mental breakdown or not, the Lord has brought me this far and restored my mind through some good medicine.

The Lord is still using that medicine today to help me to live a good, normal life.

I thank my Lord and Savior Jesus Christ for sparing my life and giving me a chance to share my testimony with you about what He brought me through.

I lost my mind, but I didn't know that I had lost my mind.

I lost my mind and reality couldn't find me.

I lost my mind and time couldn't find me.

I lost my mind and I couldn't find it.

I lost my mind and no human being could find it.

Only my Lord Jesus Christ could find my lost mind, and He found it because He knew where it was.

I am so glad that Jesus gave me my mind back through the good medicine that He inspired the doctors to give to me.

In some ways, my mind is so much better today than before I lost it when I was about 19 years old and in the military.

There is nothing Jesus Christ can't do.

Jesus can make the impossible possible in my life and in your life.

Many years ago, I believed that it was impossible for me to live in reality again.

When I lost my mind, reality left me behind and I was in an unrealistic state of mind.

It was like being blind and I could not see where I was going in my life.

I know today that the Lord winked His eye at my ignorance that may have played a part in me losing my mind, because I believe that if I had not used the illegal drugs I would never have lost my mind.

I am no better than anyone else who may have lost their mind.

It's like an unsolved mystery why some people lose their minds and never get them back again.

I can't question the Lord as to why He allowed me to lose my mind many years ago when I was very young, but I am so happy today that I can see the full strength of reality in my life.

The Lord has restored my mental powers through good medicine that I still take today.

Good medicine is from the Lord, who gives scientists the wisdom and knowledge to create good medicine to help me and you get well if it is in God's will.

It was in God's will for the medicine to work for me.

God is the best doctor in the medical field all around the world every day.

God is the best psychiatrist, psychologist, surgeon, and scientist all around the world every day.

It's the Lord God who gives everyone in the medical field wisdom, knowledge, and experience to use for His glory and not to get the glory and praise for themselves.

I truly thank God for using those professional people in the medical field, even when some of those doctors, psychiatrists, psychologists, surgeons, and scientists can sometimes do people more harm than good.

God's son, Jesus Christ, is the only one who can heal our sins and our sick souls.

Having a sick soul is the worst kind of sickness in this world every day.

I had once lost my mind, but the Lord didn't let me die in my sins for my soul to be lost — that would be forevermore worse than losing my mind.

It's a miracle to me today that I am well enough in my mind to write about my bad experiences and to share them with others.

I am doing what the Lord wants me to do, which is to help others who may not understand what it's like to lose your mind.

I am doing what the Lord wants me to do by not judging those who have lost their minds.

I didn't ever think that I would lose my mind, but it happened to me.

Today, though, I am a living miracle because of my Lord Jesus Christ.

I Want to be Caught Up in You, O Lord

I want to be caught up in You, O Lord, not caught up in myself.

I want to be caught up in You, O Lord, not caught up in anyone else.

I want to be caught up in You, O Lord, not caught up in what is going on in this world.

I want to be caught up in You, O Lord, not caught up in in the church.

I want to be caught up in You, O Lord, not caught up in material things.

I want to be caught up in You, O Lord, not caught up in how You are blessing me.

I want to be caught up in You, O Lord, not caught up in the spiritual gifts you have given me.

I want to be caught up in You, O Lord, not caught up in temporary things.

I want to be caught up in You, my Lord and Savior Jesus Christ, who is eternal for me to stay caught up in and never get disappointed.

From a Long Ways In

O Lord, You brought me from a long ways in showing Your mercy on me.

O Lord, You brought me from a long ways in cleansing me from my past sins.

O Lord, You brought me from a long ways in having faith in You.

O Lord, You brought me from a long ways in worshipping You.

O Lord, You brought me from a long ways in putting my trust in You.

O Lord, You brought me from a long ways in holding onto You.

O Lord, You brought me from a long ways in keeping my eyes on You.

O Lord, You brought me from a long ways in praying to You.

O Lord, You brought me from a long ways in giving testimonies about what You brought me through.

O Lord, You brought me from a long ways in going through trials for Your holy name sake.

O Lord, You brought me from a long ways in confessing and repenting of my sins unto You.

O Lord, You brought me from a long ways in keeping Your Sabbath day holy unto You.

O Lord, You brought me from a long ways in Your amazing grace.

O Lord, You brought me from a long ways in denying myself and picking up my cross to follow You.

O Lord, You brought me from a long ways in keeping me in my right mind.

O Lord, You brought me from a long ways in keeping me in good health.

O Lord, You brought me from a long ways in eating Your spiritual meat.

O Lord, You brought me from a long ways in assembling together with my spiritual brothers and sisters in the household of faith to worship You and give You all the glory and praise.

O Lord, You brought me from a long ways in loving You and keeping Your Commandments.

O Lord, You brought me from a long ways in having a relationship with You.

O Lord, You brought me from a long ways in using my spiritual gifts to edify the church that You are the head of.

O Lord, You brought me from a long ways in spiritually maturing in You.

O Lord, You brought me from a long ways in not laying up my treasures in the world.

O Lord, You brought me from a long ways in not making this world my home.

O Lord, You brought me from a long ways in yielding to Your Holy Spirit.

O Lord, You brought me from a long ways in not holding grudges.

O Lord, You brought me from a long ways in loving everybody the same.

O Lord, You brought me from a long ways in waiting on You to work things out in my life.

O Lord, You brought me from a long ways in setting me free from the devil's lies.

O Lord, You brought me from a long ways in giving me the victory over my obstacles in life.

O Lord, You brought me from a long ways in keeping me alive to see this day for me to give You the honor, glory and praise.

I Put My Faith in You, O Lord

I put my faith in You, O Lord, that You will give me the strength to get through this day.

I put my faith in You, O Lord, that You will supply all of my needs throughout this day.

I put my faith in You, O Lord, that You will not leave me or forsake me throughout this day.

I put my faith in You, O Lord, that You will answer my prayers.

I put my faith in You, O Lord, that You will keep Your promises to me.

I put my faith in You, O Lord, that You will not allow the devil to tempt me with more than what I can bear.

I put my faith in You, O Lord, that You will be for me and not against me.

I put my faith in You, O Lord, that You will help me to love You and keep Your Commandments.

Help Me to Not Go Back There

O Lord, help me to not go back there and hold grudges against the people who hurt my heart.

O Lord, help me to not go back there and talk bad about the people who used me.

O Lord, help me to not go back there and get revenge against the people who did me wrong.

O Lord, help me to not go back there and talk bad to the people who talked bad to me.

O Lord, help me to not go back there to the bad things that happened to me.

I can truly thank You for not letting the bad things kill me.

My Lord and Savior Jesus Christ, You didn't go back there to get revenge at the Pharisees for telling lies about You.

My Lord and Savior Jesus Christ, You didn't go back there to kill the Roman soldiers who nailed You on the cross.

O Lord, help me to be more forgiving, like You.

You Give Me Strength

O Lord, You give me strength in my mind to help keep my thoughts in line with Your holy word that is good for me all the time.

O Lord, You give me strength in my heart to keep my feelings in line with Your holy word that is deep, eternal truth for me who is a chief among sinners.

O Lord, You give me strength in my body to be Your holy temple according to Your holy word.

I seek to do right for Your service, O Lord.

O Lord, You give me strength in my life so I can live my life according to Your holy word that shows me Your will that will always bless my life.

You Winked Your Eye

O Lord, You winked Your eye at my ignorance when I had no knowledge of Your holy word.

O Lord, You winked Your eye at my ignorance when I didn't know a lot of right from wrong.

O Lord, You winked Your eye at my ignorance when I was living in the darkness of my sins.

O Lord, You winked Your eye at my ignorance when I made a lot of bad choices.

O Lord, You winked Your eye at my ignorance when I still had to suffer for living in my sins.

O Lord, You winked Your eye at my ignorance when I still had to suffer for making bad choices.

O Lord, You winked Your eye at my ignorance when I still had to suffer for not yielding to Your Holy Spirit.

O Lord, You winked Your eye at my ignorance and gave me a second chance to not die in my sins.

I Hear Your Voice

I hear Your voice, O Lord, in my mind.

You tell me to love and obey You all the time.

I hear Your voice, O Lord, in my heart.

You tell me that You are always near to me and not far away.

I hear Your voice, O Lord, in my life.

You tell me to live my life unto You, my Lord Jesus Christ.

I hear Your voice, O Lord, throughout the day.

You tell me that You number my days, regardless of what anyone says with their ifs and buts.

I hear Your voice, O Lord, in Your holy word.

You tell me that You so loved me first, even when I didn't love You or truly care to know You.

You are Worth Waiting For

O Lord, You are worth waiting for, even if it takes years for You to give me victory over the bad things in my life.

O Lord, I want to wait for You because I am tired of doing things I regret because I did them my own way.

O Lord, I need to wait for You, because I am tired of messing things up in my life.

O Lord, You are worth waiting on because You give me peace.

O Lord, I have taken some things in my own hands and I am surely paying for it the hard way now.

O Lord, You let me know that waiting for You is the right thing to do every day.

O Lord, I want to wait for You because life is too short to keep making the same mistakes over and over again.

Waiting for You, my Lord and Savior Jesus Christ, will keep me from making the same mistakes over and over again.

O Lord, You are always worth waiting for, because You can surely work things out for me no matter what.

I have done some things without waiting for You, O Lord, and it caught up with me and I regret it.

You are worth waiting for, O Lord, and I thank You for helping me to see the light.

True Happiness

Having faith in You, O Lord, gives me true happiness.

Trusting You, O Lord, gives me true happiness.

Loving You, O Lord, gives me true happiness.

Holding onto You, O Lord, gives me true happiness.

Praying to You, O Lord, gives me true happiness.

Material things can't give me true happiness.

This world can't give me true happiness.

Only You, My Lord and Savior Jesus Christ, can give me true happiness.

Being saved in You, O Lord, gives me true happiness.

Keeping my mind on You, O Lord, gives me true happiness.

Being strong in You, O Lord, gives me true happiness.

Having a relationship with You, O Lord, gives me true happiness.

Putting my hopes in You, O Lord, gives me true happiness.

Pouring Out My Heart

Pouring Out my heart unto You, my Lord, will strengthen my faith in You.

Pouring Out my heart unto You, my Lord, will bring tears to my eyes.

Pouring Out my heart unto You, my Lord, will draw me closer to You.

Pouring Out my heart unto You, my Lord, will open my eyes to see more of Your truth.

Pouring Out my heart unto You, my Lord, is a wonderful experience.

Pouring Out my heart unto You, my Lord, will humble me more and more.

Pouring Out my heart unto You, my Lord, lifts me up and helps me to keep my eyes on You.

Pouring Out my heart unto You, my Lord, helps me to love and obey You.

Your Holy Spirit, O Lord

There was a time in my life when I wasn't a Christian and I had some demons in me.

Those demons controlled my life and caused me to feel so hopeless.

When I wasn't a Christian, the Lord was so good to me to bring me this far in His goodness for me to confess and repent of my sins and give my heart to Him.

You gave me Your Holy Spirit, O Lord, for me to love You and love my spiritual brothers and sisters in the church, as well as everybody else.

Your Holy Spirit, O Lord, causes me to feel very sorrowful about living in rebellion against You many years ago.

Your Holy Spirit, O Lord, brings tears to my eyes when I feel the power of Your Holy Spirit, O Lord, in the prayers and in some of my spiritual brothers and sisters.

It makes my heart glad to know that I have spiritual brothers and sisters who love You, O Lord.

I need your Holy Spirit, O Lord, to live in me who would die so fragile and hopeless without You, O Lord, in my life.

Your Holy Spirit, O Lord, shows me the truth about myself and the truth about others who need Your Holy Spirit, O Lord, to help them to live right unto You.

Your Holy Spirit, O Lord, nurtures my broken mind and feeds it with Your holy word to strengthen my mind to think on You, O Lord, who is the great healer of broken minds and broken hearts.

Your Holy Spirit, O Lord, takes my broken prayers up to You and Your Holy Spirit will fix my broken prayers so they are suitable for You, O Lord, to answer them.

Without Your Holy Spirit in my life, I am better off never being born just like Judas was better off never being born for betraying You, my Lord and Savior Jesus Christ.

It's a Miracle to Me

It's a miracle to me, O Lord, that You can use a messed-up person like me.

I know, O Lord, that I don't deserve to be used by You.

I know that all of my righteousness is like filthy rags to you, O Lord, when I can believe that my righteousness is so good in my eyes.

Who am I to believe that I deserve You, O Lord, to answer my prayers.

It's a miracle to me, O Lord, that you brought me this far when some of my loved ones have departed from the land of the living.

I truly deserve to be in the grave that You, O Lord, saved me from so I could see this day.

O Lord, who am I to ever take You for granted in any kind of way.

It's a miracle to me, O Lord, that you see who I can become in Your holy and righteous name.

O Lord, I don't want to do my will because that will surely make me selfish, but Your holy will is freedom and sets me free from my own will that will put me in bondage every day.

It's a miracle to me, O Lord, that You still love me when I don't always love You or trust You to always be there for me.

I know, O Lord, that I am guilty of doubting that You will bring me through what I can't bring myself through.

It's a miracle to me, O Lord, that You never gave up on me when I had given up on You to chase behind this world that greatly disappointed me when I caught up with it.

It's a miracle to me, O Lord, that You didn't allow the devil to destroy me in my sins when I turned my back on You.

I Had Completely Forgotten

I have two little house dogs that I let outside in the fenced-in backyard.

One day in the late afternoon, I was upstairs in my townhouse talking on the phone.

I talked on the phone until it got dark outside.

As I was talking on the phone, I heard my little girl dog barking.

I paid her no mind, because I thought that she was barking because she heard some noise outside.

As I continued to talk on the phone, my little girl dog kept on barking.

I just didn't pay any attention to her as I talked on the phone for about two hours.

Then I heard someone knock on my front door while my dog was barking, so I walked down the stairs and looked out my kitchen window.

I saw my next-door neighbor standing in my front yard as his wife knocked on my door.

I turned on my front porch light and then I opened the door.

That young woman told me that she had heard my dog barking a lot and she thought that something was wrong.

She asked me if I was all right.

I told her that I was all right, and then I thanked her for checking on me.

After I closed the door, I went to check on my two little dogs that I thought were in their kennels.

When I looked in the kennels, I saw only one of my little dogs.

I figured out right away that my little girl dog was barking a lot because my little boy dog was outside in the backyard.

I had forgotten that I let him outside in the cold weather.

When I finally let him in the house, he was so happy to come back inside.

My little boy dog has a loud bark and I didn't hear him bark at all during the whole time that he was outside in the backyard.

I truly thank the Lord that he has a fur coat that kept him from getting too cold.

Sometimes, we can completely forget some things, but the Lord is so good and merciful that He will not make us regret it if it's in His will.

Some people have completely forgotten something and it caused some fatalities.

We just can't know why God allows a baby to be left in a hot car to die because a parent completely forgot to take the baby out of the car.

We can't question God and blame God when bad things happen.

I Took a Lot of Chances

I took a lot of chances that could have caused me to lose my life, because I was young and ignorant in many ways.

I took a lot of chances and didn't give it a second thought.

I took a lot of chances and didn't care.

A lot of those chances I took were caused by the way I lived my life.

It's a miracle that I am still alive today.

I now know what a fool I was.

I know the right way to live now, and I don't want to ever again do those foolish things I used to do.

I thank the Lord for giving me a chance to live for Him and to know His holy word.

I know today that taking chances is not always a good thing to do.

The Lord didn't let my chances take my life.

My eyes are open today, and now I can see the chances I take.

The chances I take today are good because I live my life unto the Lord.

When I took a chance with Jesus Christ, my Lord, it was the best chance that I've ever taken.

I have no regrets at all.

Thanks to Jesus, I've learned to wise up and not take any more bad chances that I'm aware of.

I took a lot of chances when I was young and inexperienced with a lot of things in life.

Jesus has paid my price for the bad chances I took.

Tell the Truth

Thirty-four years ago, I was married to my first wife who is now deceased because of breast cancer that she had about twenty-two years ago.

Before I married her, I had no knowledge that she was manic depressive so I didn't seek any marriage counseling before I married her.

My first wife didn't like taking her medication for her manic depression and she would be violent toward me to the point that I got arrested and put in jail for defending myself because she was abusing me.

I was sentenced to four months in jail, and I had so much more peace there than I had living under the same roof with my first wife.

When I was in jail, I made friends with some of the inmates and we talked about the Lord and shared bible scriptures with one another.

I only had about three weeks left in jail when I witnessed two other inmates fighting on the indoor basketball court.

The correctional officer in the ward I was in wanted to know who started the fight.

The Lord put it in my heart to speak up and tell the truth about who started the fight.

A few days after I told the truth, I was transferred from minimum security to a maximum-security in jail.

In the maximum-security jail, I was placed in a cell with a murderer.

The whole cell block was filled with murderers and other violent criminals.

I know that the Lord was with me because no one in the cell block put me in harm's way or danger.

The Lord had truly given me the strength and the courage to not be afraid of those murderers and other violent criminals.

I was not afraid to talk about the Lord and His holy word when I was placed in the maximum-security jail cell.

I spoke plain and told the truth in the minimum-security jail about the fight that I witnessed.

Telling the truth caused me to be placed in the maximum-security facility.

The Lord put it in my heart to tell the truth about who started the fight on the basketball court.

Before I spoke up and told the truth, the inmate who did not start the fight was accused of starting it.

If telling the truth causes you to make enemies, then it is worth it because if God is for you then who can be against you for telling the truth?

If I had not obeyed the Lord, who put it in my heart to tell the truth, then there was no telling who else would have had the conscious to tell the truth.

It's sometimes difficult to tell the truth, whether you're locked up in jail or free in society every day.

The Lord foreknew that me telling the truth would encourage another jail inmate to tell the truth too.

Real, true bondage is telling lies, even if you and I are free as a bird flying up in the sky.

Not standing up for the truth, especially when it comes to God's holy word, is surely living a lie, whether you're locked up in jail or living free in society.

The devil meant it for my bad when I got locked up in jail for defending myself and trying to get away from my abusive first wife who refused to take her medication for her manic depression.

The Lord used me being locked up in jail for my good so I would stand up and tell the truth with boldness about who started the fight on the indoor basketball court.

I have no regrets about telling the truth, even though I was placed in the maximum-security jail where the Lord protected me from the worst kinds of criminals when I was there.

Telling the truth is freedom, even when you're locked up in jail where there is no freedom.

Telling the truth is freedom from the bondage of keeping silent about what you witness.

Keeping silent about the truth is like telling a lie, whether you and I are living free in society or we're locked up in jail.

True freedom is telling the truth.

The Lord loves the truth every day, and the truth sets us free from the devil's lies, even if you and I are locked up in jail.

Even though I was locked up in jail, I felt true freedom for telling the truth in that bondage environment where the Lord caused the worst kinds of criminals to make peace with me.

When I gave my life to the Lord, my mind was made up to tell the truth and live the truth unto the Lord who knew that my motives and intentions were true in my marriage to my first wife regardless of her manic-depressive disorder that was hard on her as well as being hard on me too.

I've learned that even in troubled times it is always good to tell the truth, even under hard circumstances in our lives.

The Lord hates a lying tongue and it will not go unpunished in the Lord's eyesight.

Telling the truth in love is splendor to the Lord, even if you and I are locked up in jail for doing something wrong that we did not plan to do.

When Jesus lived here on earth, He always told the truth even though the scribes and Pharisees did not believe Him and had caused Jesus to be crucified because they believed He was telling lies.

Jesus never kept silent about the truth that He foreknew would set people free from the devil's lies.

The devil didn't want anyone to believe that Jesus was the living truth sent from heaven by God to redeem all human beings back to God.

Jesus was never afraid to tell the truth to sinners being who we are.

Jesus Christ is the way, the truth and the life for you and me to tell the truth that has no wrongs for anyone not to tell the truth.

No matter what we do, the Lord will forgive us if we truly repent unto Him.

In My Mind and in My Heart

I believe in my mind that You, Lord Jesus, are the Son of God, and I need to love you, O Lord, in my heart.

I believe in my mind that You, Lord Jesus, are the way, the truth and the life, but in my heart, I need to trust You.

I believe in my mind that You, Lord Jesus, do answer my prayers, but in my heart, I need to wait on You to answer my prayers.

I believe in my mind that You, Lord Jesus, cannot fail me, but in my heart, I need to claim my victory in You.

I believe in my mind that You, Lord Jesus, will forgive me of my sins, but in my heart, I need to confess and repent of my sins unto You.

I believe in my mind that You, Lord Jesus, can cleanse me from my sins and save me from my sins, but in my heart, I need to not hold onto my sins.

I believe in my mind that You, Lord Jesus, will not condemn my heart but in my heart, I need to not condemn myself.

I believe in my mind that You, Lord Jesus, brought me this far in my life, but in my heart, I need to let go of all the wrongs that I have done.

I believe in my mind that You, Lord Jesus, will never change on me, but in my heart, I need to not change on You.

I believe in my mind that You, Lord Jesus, are the word of God, but in my heart, I need to live my life unto You who speaks the holy word.

I believe in my mind that You, Lord Jesus, are coming back again, but in my heart, I need to pray and watch and live my life like You could come back again on any day.

What I believe in my mind and in my heart can be different, but You, Lord Jesus, truly know my mind and my heart to bring them on one accord in You.

My mind and my heart must come together to please You, my Lord and Savior Jesus Christ, who has given me a mind that believes in You and a heart that loves You.

My Lord Jesus Christ, You gave me a mind to choose right from wrong and You gave me a heart to live right from wrong.

If I don't choose you, Lord Jesus, in my mind every day, then I won't live for You in my heart day after day.

I can't separate my mind and my heart from You, my Lord Jesus, and believe that my life is in harmony with You.

O, my Lord and Savior Jesus Christ, the demons believe that You are the Son of God who kicked them out of heaven because they stopped loving You.

The mind can be very powerful.

It can cause you and me to believe that we can walk on the water just like Jesus walked on water.

Peter walked on water until he began to look at the rugged waves fearfully.

What can a mind really accomplish without the heart?

What can the heart really accomplish without the mind?

The mind and heart must go hand in hand with the Lord, so we can uplift and glorify His holy name inside the church and outside the church.

Please Don't Shake Me Out of the Church

O Lord, please don't shake me out of the church because I want to believe in You every day.

O Lord, please don't shake me out of the church because I want to put my hope in You every day.

O Lord, please don't shake me out of the church because I want to worship You every day.

O Lord, please don't shake me out of the church because I want to put my trust in You every day.

O Lord, please don't shake me out of the church because I want to deny myself and pick up my cross and follow You every day.

O Lord, please don't shake me out of the church because I want to love You and keep your Commandments every day.

O Lord, please don't shake me out of the church because I want to have a relationship with You every day.

O Lord, please don't shake me out of the church because I want to keep my eyes on You every day.

O Lord, please don't shake me out of the church because I want to hold onto You every day.

O Lord, please don't shake me out of the church because I want to give You all of my heart every day.

O Lord, please don't shake me out of the church because I want to confess and repent of my sins unto You every day.

O Lord, please don't shake me out of the church because I want to be saved in You every day.

O Lord, please don't shake me out of the church because I want to live my life unto You every day.

O Lord, please don't shake me out of the church because I want to glorify and praise Your holy name every day.

O Lord, please don't shake me out of the church because I want to be a witness of You every day.

O Lord, please don't shake me out of the church because I want to be like You every day.

O Lord, please don't shake me out of the church because I want to know Your holy word every day.

O Lord, please don't shake me out of the church because I want to live by Your holy word every day.

O Lord, please don't shake me out of the church because I want to be watchful every day to see You coming back again on the clouds of glory one day.

O Lord, please don't shake me out of the church because I want to keep myself humble unto You every day.

O Lord, please don't shake me out of the church because I want to show reverence to You every day.

O Lord, please don't shake me out of the church because I want to be filled with Your holy spirit every day.

O Lord, You Brought Me

O Lord, You brought me through the dark tunnels in my life.

O Lord, You brought me through the dark caves in my life.

O Lord, You brought me through the storms in my life.

O Lord, You brought me through the hurricanes in my life.

O Lord, You brought me through the tornadoes in my life.

O Lord, You brought me through the tidal waves in my life.

O Lord, You brought me through the flood waters in my life.

O Lord, You brought me through the wildfires in my life.

O Lord, You brought me through the unpredictability in my life.

O Lord, You brought me through the car crashes in my life.

O Lord, You brought me through the heat waves in my life.

O Lord, You brought me through the lion's den in my life.

O Lord, You brought me through the snow blizzards in my life.

O Lord, You brought me from a mighty long ways in my life.

O Lord, You brought me through the frost bites in my life.

O Lord, You brought me through the trench foots in my life.

O Lord, You brought me through the spider bites in my life.

O Lord, You brought me through the viruses in my life.

O Lord, You brought me through the heartaches in my life.

O Lord, You brought me through the tears in my life.

O Lord, You brought me through the wrinkles in my life.

O Lord, You brought me through the sores in my life.

O Lord, You brought me through the broken glass in my life.

O Lord, You brought me through the failures in my life.

O Lord, You brought me through the hopelessness in my life.

O Lord, You brought me through the defeats in my life.

O Lord, You brought me through the droughts in my life.

O Lord, You brought me through the famines in my life.

O Lord, You brought me from a mighty long ways in my life.

O Lord, You brought me through the rain forests in my life.

O Lord, You brought me through the insomnia in my life.

O Lord, You brought me through the earthquakes in my life.

O Lord, You brought me through the tsunamis in my life.

O Lord, You brought me from a mighty long ways that takes my mind up into Your miraculous spiritual heights and lets me know that I didn't bring myself this far to see this day that I don't deserve to see no matter what good things that I do.

O Lord, Help Me

O Lord, help me to live right by the truth of Your holy word.

I know, O Lord, You give me Your holy spirit to help me to remember what I need to know about You, my Lord and Savior Jesus Christ.

O Lord, my soul cries out for Your help that I need twenty-four hours around the clock.

O Lord, help me not to take even one second of Your love, mercy and grace for granted as if I am self-made and don't need You.

O Lord, help me to love you with all of my mind, heart, soul and strength that is always good for me to do.

I don't have to feel insecure, because You, O Lord, will always be there for me on my good days and bad days.

O Lord, help me to always know that I didn't bring myself this far in my life, because it's You who has brought me this far in my life.

O Lord, help me to give You my all.

I know I don't have to worry about whether my all is good enough to please you, O Lord, because You always know the limit of my all.

Only You can judge when my all may not be good enough; human beings can't judge this.

O Lord, help me to listen to and obey the voice of Your holy spirit who will lead and guide me into all the truth about You, my Lord and Savior Jesus Christ.

O Lord, help me to love everybody and to treat everybody right, even my enemies who can't do more harm to me that what You allow.

O Lord, help me to fully trust You and not trust me, who is not perfect and makes mistakes.

O Lord, help me to live my life unto You, who gives life its true meaning to exist beyond death that is only temporary.

You, O Lord, are the eternal life to give to me for being saved in You, O Lord

I Have Some Rascal in Me

I know, O Lord, that I have some rascal in me, but I am so glad that You see some good in me to use me to uplift Your holy name.

I know, O Lord, that I have some rascal in me, but I am so glad that You love me and want to save me from my sins.

I know, O Lord, that I have some rascal in me, but I am so glad that You found me to be fit to deny myself and pick up my cross and follow you.

I know, O Lord, that I have some rascal in me, but I am so glad, O Lord, that You didn't give up on me who was so lost in my sins.

I know, O Lord, that I have some rascal in me, but I am so glad that You brought me this far in my life so a rascal like me can confess and repent of my sins unto You, my Lord and Savior Jesus Christ.

I know, O Lord, that I have some rascal thoughts, but I am so glad that You will enter into my mind for me to think of you, O Lord.

I know, O Lord, that I can say some rascal words, but I am so glad that You will speak through me with Your holy words of everlasting discipline.

I know, O Lord, that I can do some rascal deeds, but I am so glad that You will give me Your holy spirit for me to do right by You.

I know, O Lord, that I have some rascal in me, but I am so glad that You want to cleanse me from my rascal sins and save my soul from being lost in this rascal world.

I Never Knew What it was Like

I never knew what it was like to have my father in my life, which had void in it because my father wasn't in my life.

I am sixty-six years old, and today and I still feel the pain from the absence of my father in my life.

One day, I was watching an old western drama on TV about a boy not knowing who his father was until he met his father, who didn't welcome him with open arms right away.

His father was also broken from being in prison for robbing a bank.

The boy and his father finally embraced each other after the boy let his father know how much he missed having his father in his life.

The boy and his father felt the pain from those words spoken by the boy, while at the same time they were set free from the pain when they embraced each other with joy for being relieved from missing each other for years.

When I watched the boy and his father embrace each other, I felt like I wanted to cry because of thinking about my father not being in my life when I was a little boy.

As I grew up into an adult, I finally met my father and talked to him and this gave me great relief from his absence in my life.

My father is deceased now, but I still feel the pain from his absence, especially when I see child actors portraying children who are heartbroken due to the absence of their father in their lives.

I know today that I am so blessed to have a heavenly Father who will never leave me or forsake me.

I just didn't know that God was always with me when I was a child.

I never knew what it was like to have my biological father in my life when I was a child, but today I know what it's like to have my heavenly Father, God, in my life.

Even if my biological father was in my life when I was a child, he would not have been a better father to me than my heavenly Father, God, who no earthly father can out-do in providing for my daily needs.

Carry Me Through

My Lord Jesus, I need You to carry me through my disappointments because I have no strength to walk on my own through anything that disappoints me.

My Lord Jesus, I need You to carry me through my thoughts because I have no strength to walk on my own through anything that I think.

My Lord Jesus, I need You to carry me through my words that I say because I have no strength to walk on my own through whatever I say.

My Lord Jesus, I need You to carry me through my grief because I have no strength to walk on my own through my tears.

My Lord Jesus, I need You to carry me through my bad days because I have no strength to walk on my own through anything that goes wrong in the day.

My Lord Jesus, I need You to carry me through my heart because I have no strength to walk on my own through my motives and intentions that can catch me off guard and make me deceive myself into doing my own will instead of Your holy will, my Lord and Savior Jesus Christ.

My Lord Jesus, I need You to carry me though my free will choices because I have no strength to walk on my own through my free will choices that I can take for granted and make choices to live for this world that is no friend to You, my Lord Jesus, who doesn't need me who would deceive myself into believing that you need a sinner like me.

Before I Was Born

God knew my thoughts before I was born.

God knew my words before I was born.

God knew my actions before I was born.

God knew my heart before I was born.

God knew my mind before I was born.

God knew my choices that I would make before I was born.

God knew my feelings before I was born.

God knew my fears before I was born.

God knew my failures before I was born.

God knew my disappointments before I was born.

God knew my sorrows before I was born.

God knew my joy before I was born.

God knew my accomplishments before I was born.

God knew my doubts before I was born.

God knew my dreams before I was born.

God knew my hardships before I was born.

God knew my life before I was born.

God knew my destiny before I was born.

God knew everything about me before I was born.

There is nothing that God didn't know about me before I was born.

God knew my purpose in life before I was born.

God knew all of my ups and downs in life before I was born.

God knew my name before I was born.

God knew my sins before I was born.

God knew my secrets before I was born.

God knew my mistakes before I was born.

God knew my flaws before I was born.

God knew my habits before I was born.

God knew my hereditary tendencies before I was born.

God knew my motives before I was born.

God knew my intentions before I was born.

God knew my past, present and future before I was born to know nothing.

www.ingramcontent.com/pod-product-compliance
Lightning Source LLC
Chambersburg PA
CBHW071004120626
46546CB00003B/930